*They will come back, those days, and
start you dreaming,
Years after in the fall when you're away.
You may forget for years this
place, your college,
And find it in your heart
Some autumn day.*

Mary Martin '43

We have lit a candle in the wilderness which will never be extinguished.

Gunnison Memorial Chapel

ST. LAWRENCE
UNIVERSITY

Photographed by John de Visser

Black Star

HARMONY HOUSE PUBLISHERS-LOUISVILLE

Executive Editors: William Butler and William Strode
Library of Congress Catalog Number: 90-81399
Hardcover International Standard Book Number 0-916509-72-9
Printed by D.W. Friesen, Manitoba, Canada
First Edition printed Fall, 1990 by Harmony House Publishers,
P.O. Box 90, Prospect, Kentucky 40059 (502) 228-2010 / 228-4446
Copyright © 1990 by Harmony House Publishers
Photographs © copyright 1990 by John de Visser

This book or portions thereof may not be reproduced in any form without
permission of Harmony House Publishers. Photographs may not be
reproduced in any form without permission of John de Visser.

PREFACE

A number of years ago, I enjoyed a conversation with Lena Wallace Stevenson '05, on the occasion of her 100th birthday. As we spoke at her home, she had vivid memories of St. Lawrence, circa 1901-05. One aspect was particularly clear — "President Gunnison walking up on campus from Park Street with his basket on his arm." (That was before briefcases.)

Lena Stevenson was not the only alumna or alumnus frequently to bring my attention to the many images of St. Lawrence. These images form one of the strongest attachments to the institution. An alumna of 1984 recalls crisp, sunny February days. (Any graduate remembers those.) For the late Atwood Manley '16, it was the vigor of the undergraduates pursuing St. Lawrence's purposes. President Emeritus Frank Piskor said it was "the St. Lawrence family," of which there are few photos.

So, we present to the St. Lawrence family this photo essay for your pleasure and an enduring sense of place.

We are deeply indebted to Lisa Cania, director of University communications, and her staff for the diligent work in assembling this book. We also extend our appreciation to photographer John de Visser, whose skill is evident, and to Harmony House Publishers.

Frank Shields '54
Director of Alumni Relations

INTRODUCTION

"Bright is the noble edifice that is pervaded by new light." So Stuart A. Winning '22, retired University physician and longtime trustee, begins the book *The Windows of Gunnison Memorial Chapel.* We thought we would borrow this quote for the introduction of this new book, a photographic essay of St. Lawrence University. Somehow, nearly 850 years later, and in reference to an independent, liberal arts college, the quote seems right at home.

The new light. It pervades the morning in Canton, making the snow on the Avenue of the Elms appear as residual stardust from the waning night. It blushes across the sky, horizon radiant in deep pink as afternoon gives way to gentle evening. It appears through the windows of Sykes Residence or Memorial Hall, as students and faculty illuminate their offices and rooms for an evening of conversation or reading. It strikes the scarlet and brown, the blue, yellow, purple and green, of the stained glass windows in Gunnison Chapel, Richardson Hall and Herring-Cole Library. It is diffuse and mysterious through the aquarium in Bewkes Science Center, it is magical on the holiday tree standing three stories tall at the corner of the quad. The new light welcomes students outdoors for football and frisbee on the first spring day and it bonds freshmen in the quad experience on the evening before classes begin and the St. Lawrence experience awaits.

Imageries of light describe the places of St. Lawrence. But all Laurentians know that alma mater is more than scenery, however beautiful and sometimes iridescent. Imageries of light also describe the experience that is St. Lawrence. "The candle in the wilderness" is the light of wisdom breaking the darkness of ignorance. It is the light of information revealing what had been before unknown and therefore unappreciated. The ever-changing flicker of the flame, altered by every movement, reminds us that St. Lawrence is sometimes subtly, sometimes greatly changed by each of us who enters her campus.

How proper in this book to recall that light is the substance (if that's the right word) of St. Lawrence. It is light which aids or hinders the photographer

from the mission. To capture a place, to capture a people on film, the photographer must seduce the light, making it the mistress of the medium of photography. Too much light and the photograph is harsh, hurting our eyes and making us look away and abandon our hope of memory. Too little light and the photograph is dim, making us furrow our brows in search of the image and wish anxiously for a glimpse of the secret withheld. The right light recreates the moment of the photograph and reminds us of similar moments in our own hearts. The right light brings back Professor Gaines or Professor Reiff or Chairman Owen D. Young to our side, brings back the Bacheller Memorial Chimes to our ears, brings back the scent of an autumn barbeque at Phi Kap after a football game.

These days, natural light at St. Lawrence still defines our days. The sun still provides daylight, and daylight streams into classrooms, dorm rooms and offices to brighten our moods. The outdoors is important to us at St. Lawrence; its vicissitudes cause our own. When the sun shines, even through cold air, we are cheerful. But artificial light, shining from the computer terminal or manipulated by the physics majors, reminds us that we have great new resources and that we have a responsibility to use wisely the resources given us. St. Lawrence has been careful to teach such citizenship. Perhaps more than the places or the people, it is the character of the University we most value.

This book was created after a year's work so that light could be captured in every season. We hope it succeeds in evoking that character that the reader will recognize as St. Lawrence.

— *Lisa M. Cania*
Director of University Communications

A ST. LAWRENCE CHRONOLOGY

1856 Universalist Church leaders apply to New York State for a charter for a college of letters and science and a theological school; the cornerstone of College Hall, now Richardson Hall, is laid.

1857 Ebenezer Fisher is named first president of the Theologial School; local residents encourage the State Legislature to allocate $50,000 for the endowment of the University. The Legislature responds with $25,000, on the condition that this sum be equalled by the members of the University corporation; thus St. Lawrence's first successful "matching grant" results.

1859 John Stebbins Lee is named first principal, or president, of the College of Letters and Science; Thomas Jefferson Sawyer is named first president of the corporation.

1861 Olympia Brown is accepted as a student at the Theological School. She graduated in 1863 and became the first American woman to be ordained a minister; the first graduation of the students of the Theological School is held.

1865 Sarah Emma Sprague and Mary Cordelia Herrick are the first graduates of the College of Letters and Science.

1867 Martin Thatcher is elected chairman of the Board.

1868 Richmond Fisk becomes president, he also serves as chairman of the board.

1869 The first Moving Up Day, then called Tree Holiday, is held.

1871 Jonas Sheldon Conkey becomes chairman of the board.

1872 Absalom Graves Gaines becomes president.

1873 The P. D. Society, later to become a chapter of Beta Theta Pi, is the first fraternity at St. Lawrence.

1875 The Browning Society, later to become Kappa Kappa Gamma, is the first sorority.

1876 Scarlet and brown are designated the official school colors; the "Union Alumni Association" is founded.

1882 The first yearbook, entitled *The Gridiron*, is published.

1883 Arthur Guinness Rogers is elected chairman of the board.

1887 Edwin Atkins Merritt is elected chairman of the board; he serves for 29 years, the longest term of office of any chairman of the board. *The Laurentian*, an alumni and literary magazine, is published for the first time.

1888 Alpheus Baker Hervey becomes president.

1891 Poet Robert Frost visits campus and meets his future wife, Elinor White, Class of 1895.

1893 The first Freshman-Sophomore Debate begins the tradition of forensics competition at St. Lawrence.

1894 The Thelomathesian Society becomes the official student government organization.

1896 John Clarence Lee becomes president.

1897 Emily Eaton Hepburn, Class of 1886, is elected to the Board of Trustees, the first woman to sit on this governing board.

1899 Almon Gunnison becomes president; a chapter of Phi Beta Kappa is installed at St. Lawrence; first intercollegiate basketball season; buildings on campus include Herring Library, Fisher Hall, College Hall and a gymnasium.

1903 St. Lawrence affiliates with the Brooklyn Law School, an affiliation which extended until the mid-1940s.

1905 The "Great Rebellion" results in the suspension of 30-40 students. The "Rebellion" is begun after a student is reprimanded for smoking on the steps of Richardson Hall.

1906 The State School of Agriculture is founded on the St. Lawrence campus.

1911 *The Hill News* is founded as the official student newspaper.

1916 Frank Amner Gallup becomes president; Vasco Pickett Abbott is elected chairman of the board; the first Alumni Fund is launched.

1919 Ledyard Park Hale is elected chairman of the board; Richard Eddy Sykes becomes president.

1921 First Christmas Candlelight Service is held; the *St. Lawrence Songbook* is published.

1922 WCAD, the nation's first college radio station and later to become KSLU, goes on the air at St. Lawrence; first athletic "L" Club forms to honor athletes.

1924 Owen D. Young, Class of 1894, is elected chairman of the board.

1926 Gunnison Memorial Chapel is built; first intercollegiate ice hockey season.

1927 Dean Eaton Hall opens.

1929 Hepburn Hall for Chemistry is dedicated by Madame Marie Curie.

1931 Men's Residence, later Sykes Hall, opens.

1933 The New York Giants play St. Lawrence's baseball team thanks to the influence of Hal Schumacher '33, a pitcher for the Giants for many years.

1934 Millard Henry Jencks is elected chairman of the board.

1935 Laurens Hickok Seelye becomes president.

1940 Millard H. Jencks '05 becomes president.

1942 Edward John Noble is elected chairman of the board.

1945 Eugene Garrett Bewkes becomes president.

1946 The Laurentian Singers is founded.

1948 The State Education Department assumes control of the Agricultural and Technical Institute, now called Canton College of Technology.

1950 Appleton Arena is completed.

1951 Fisher Hall, home to the Theology School, is destroyed by fire.

1955 Homer Albon Vilas '13 is elected chairman of the board; Atwood Hall is dedicated as the new home to the Theology School.

1956 *Candle in the Wilderness: A Centennial History of St. Lawrence University* is published.

1958 The David B. Steinman Festival of the Arts is inaugurated.

1959 The Owen D. Young Library is dedicated.

1963 Foster Sargent Brown '30 becomes president.

1964 St. Lawrence's first international study program, in Rouen, France, is established. Nine others are to follow: Spain (1967), Kenya (1974), Austria (1975), Canada (1977), England (1978), Denmark (1980), Japan (1983), Soviet Union (1988), India (1990).

1965 Trustees vote to close the Theology School following the merger of the American Unitarian Association and the Universalist Church of America; St. Lawrence acquires Camp Canaras.

1966 St. Lawrence acquires Catamount Lodge.

1967 The first computers are installed on campus.

1968 Arthur Starratt Torrey '24 is elected chairman of the board.

1969 Frank Peter Piskor becomes president; the Associated Colleges of the St. Lawrence Valley is founded.

1970 The 4-1-4 calendar, featuring two full semesters and a short, "Winterterm" is inaugurated; St. Lawrence students vote to strike classes for two days to protest the Vietnam War and the killing of four students at Kent State University.

1973 "Enterprise St. Lawrence - A Challenge to Enrich a Heritage of Quality and Independence" capital campaign is launched; St. Lawrence wins the national riding championships for the first time. We win again in 1976, 1977, and 1981.

1976 St. Lawrence wins the national title in men's swimming.

1978 Alfred Colville Viebranz '42 is elected chairman of the board.

1980 Enterprise St. Lawrence is completed with $30 million in capital and annual funds accruing to the University.

1981 W. Lawrence Gulick becomes president.

1983 John William Hannon Jr., '44 is elected chairman of the board.

1987 Patti McGill Peterson becomes St. Lawrence's first woman president.

1988 Bruce Whitlock Benedict '60 is elected chairman of the board; all freshman students enroll in The Freshman Program; St. Lawrence wins the national title in men's wrestling.

1990 Carnegie Hall renovations completed; the Carnegie Center for International Education is dedicated; ODYsseus is dedicated in the Owen D. Young Library.

May thy fair name dwell forever
In our fondest memory,
And when college days are over,
From this Hill we've wended down,
We will love thee yet,
We'll ne'er forget the Scarlet and the Brown.

From "Alma Mater"

Carnegie Center for International Education

No volume can adequately record what is in our minds, our memories, and our hearts regarding the most effective and unselfish contributors to the life of this school. Men and women of sound learning, exploring scholarship, and fearless intellect, who instruct the young in the wisdom of the past, and guide them in freedom toward the undiscovered truths of the future.

Owen D. Young, in Preface to Candle in the Wilderness, October 1956.

From Owen D. Young Library

Students need thinking time during their university years, time free for wool-gathering, time to assimilate the knowledge "proper" with which they are bombarded, time reserved for sifting and re-sifting, for speculation and questions.

President Foster S. Brown, Inaugural Address, October 19, 1963

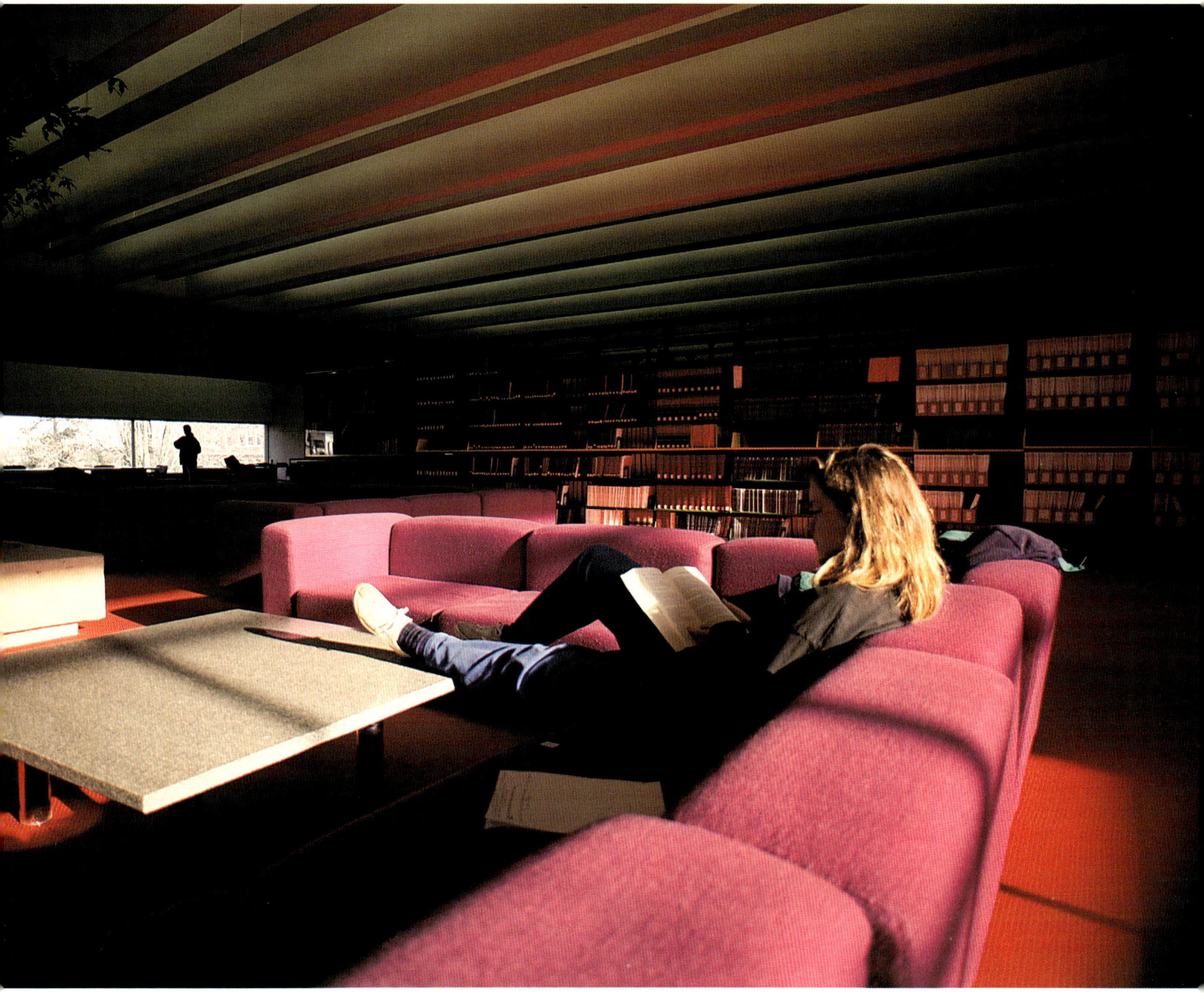

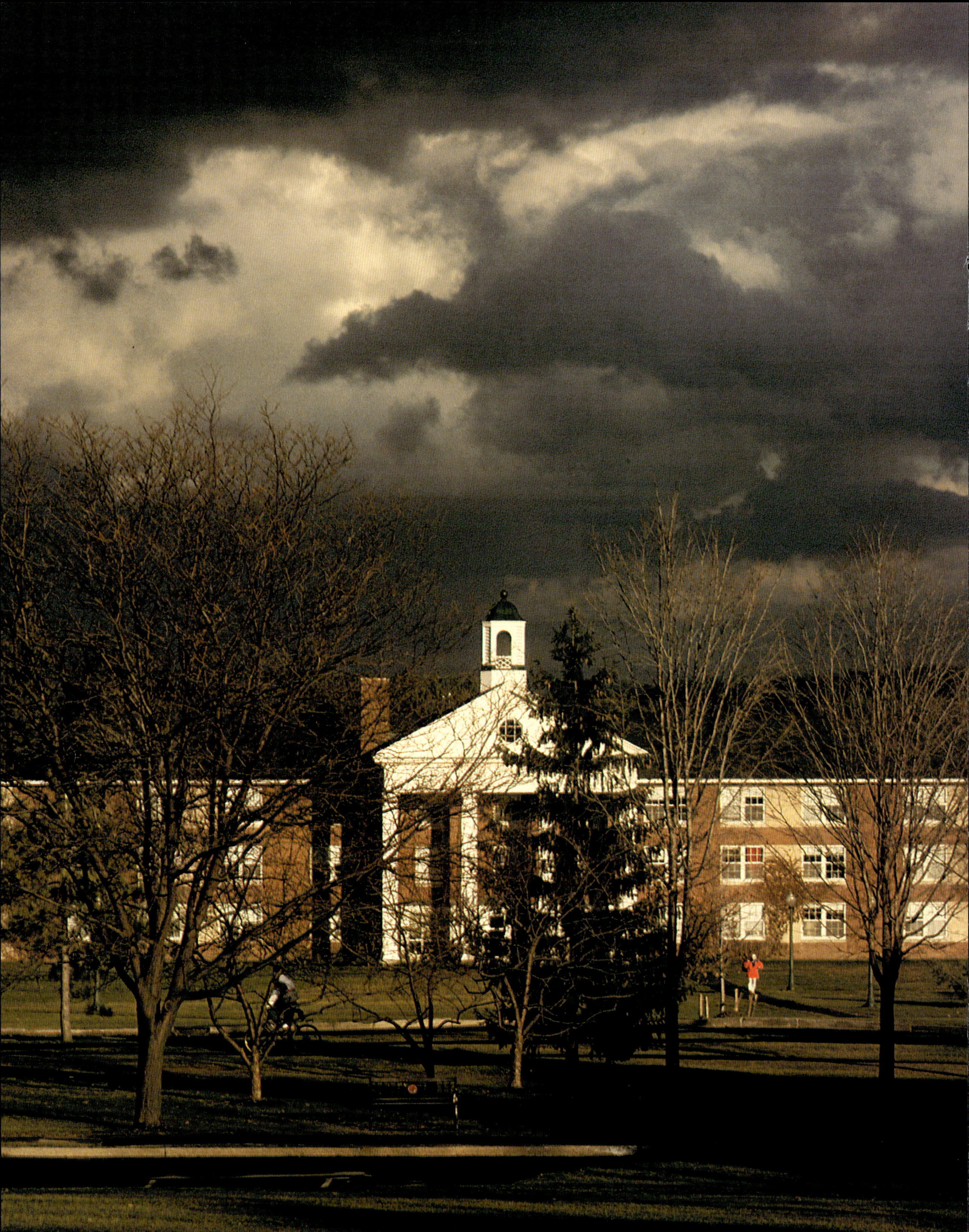

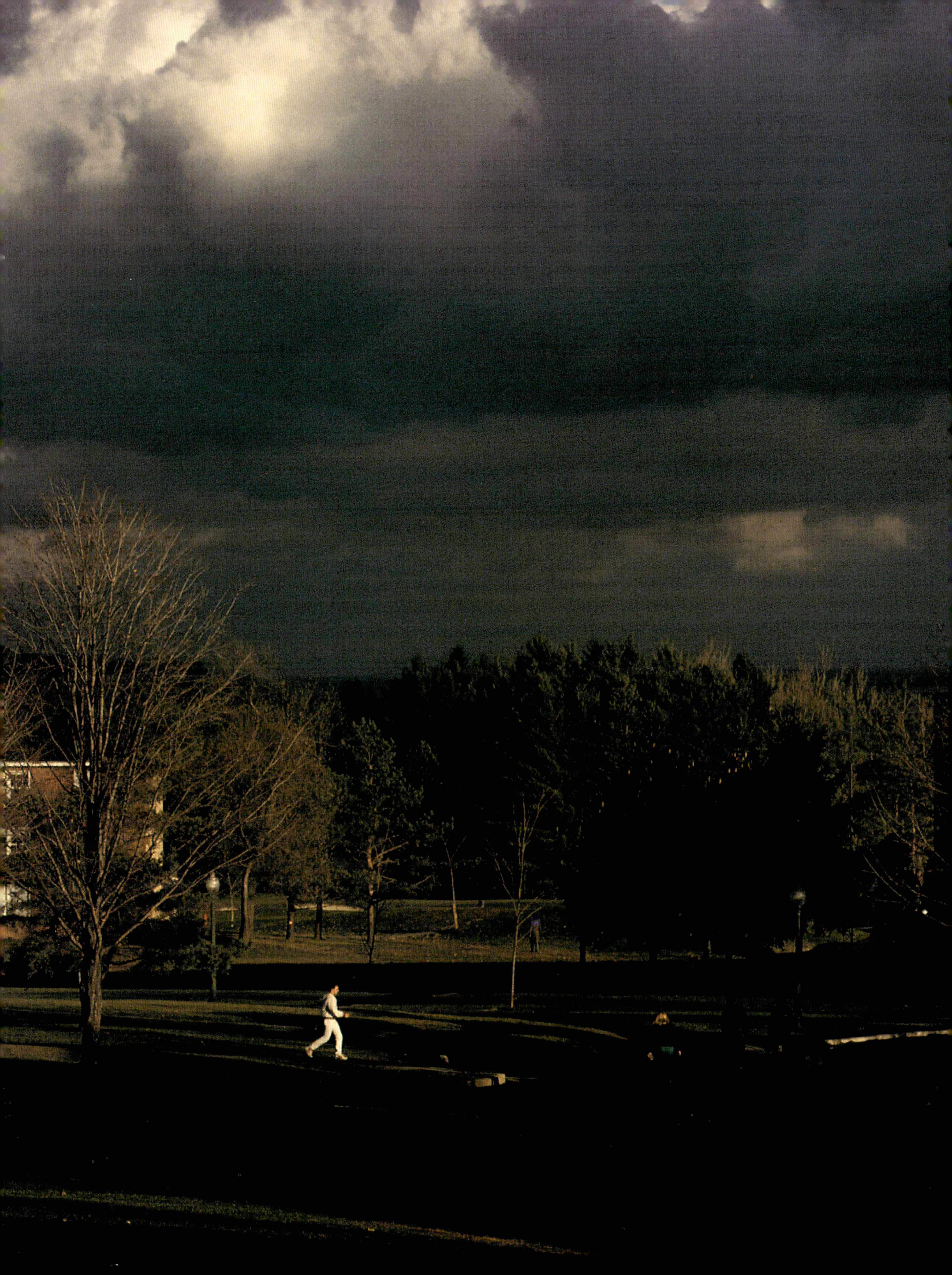

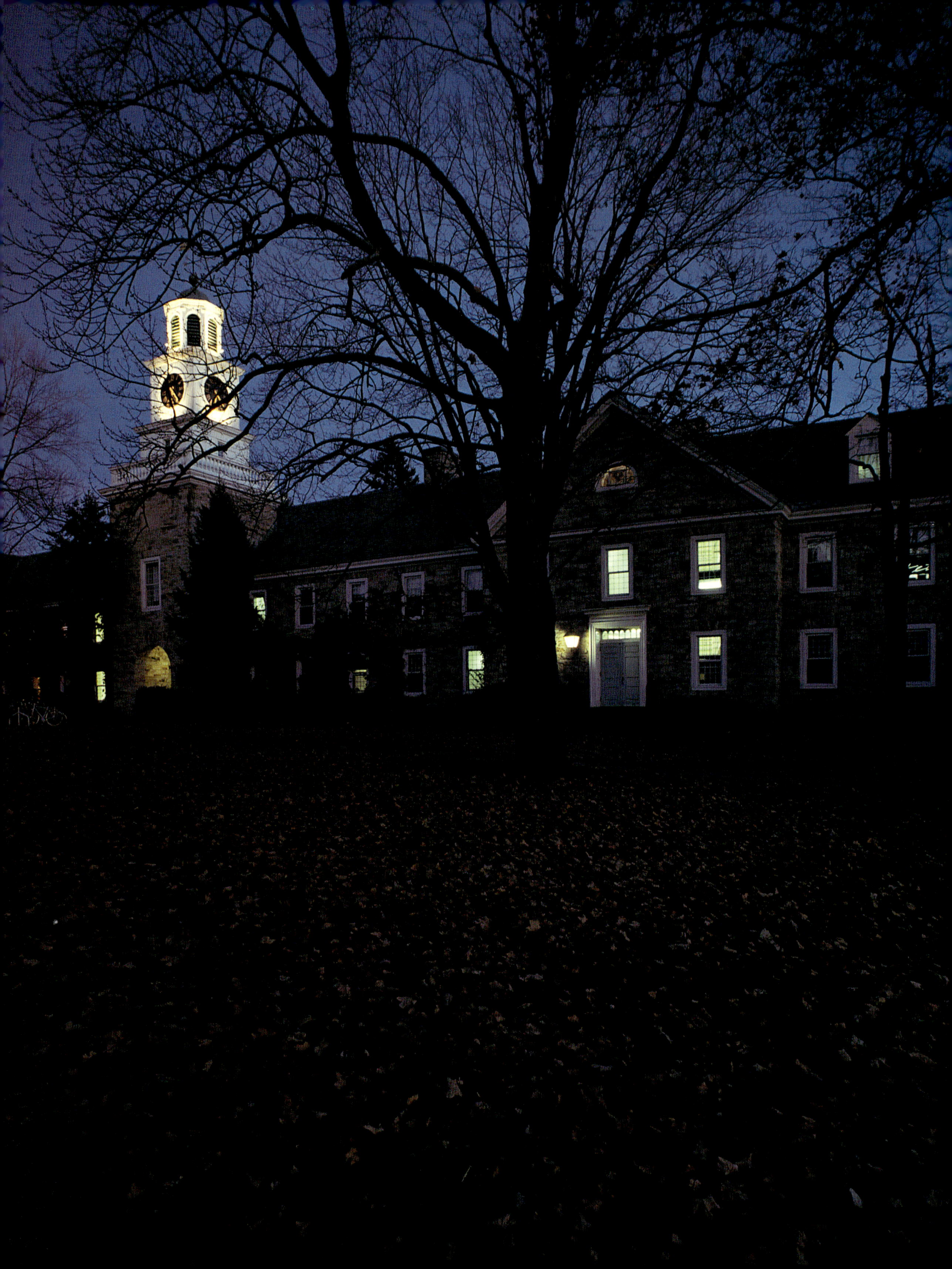

Sykes Hall

39

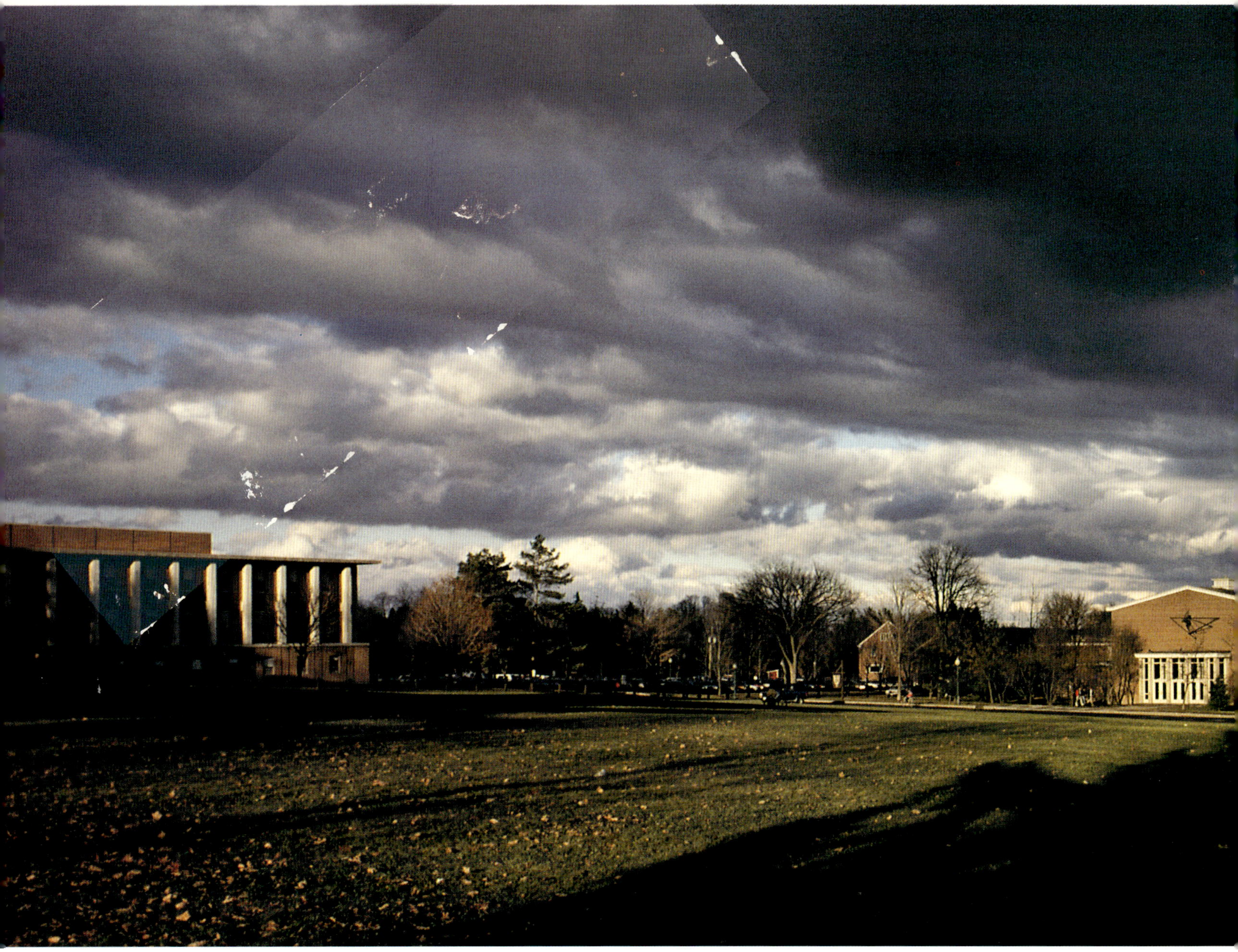

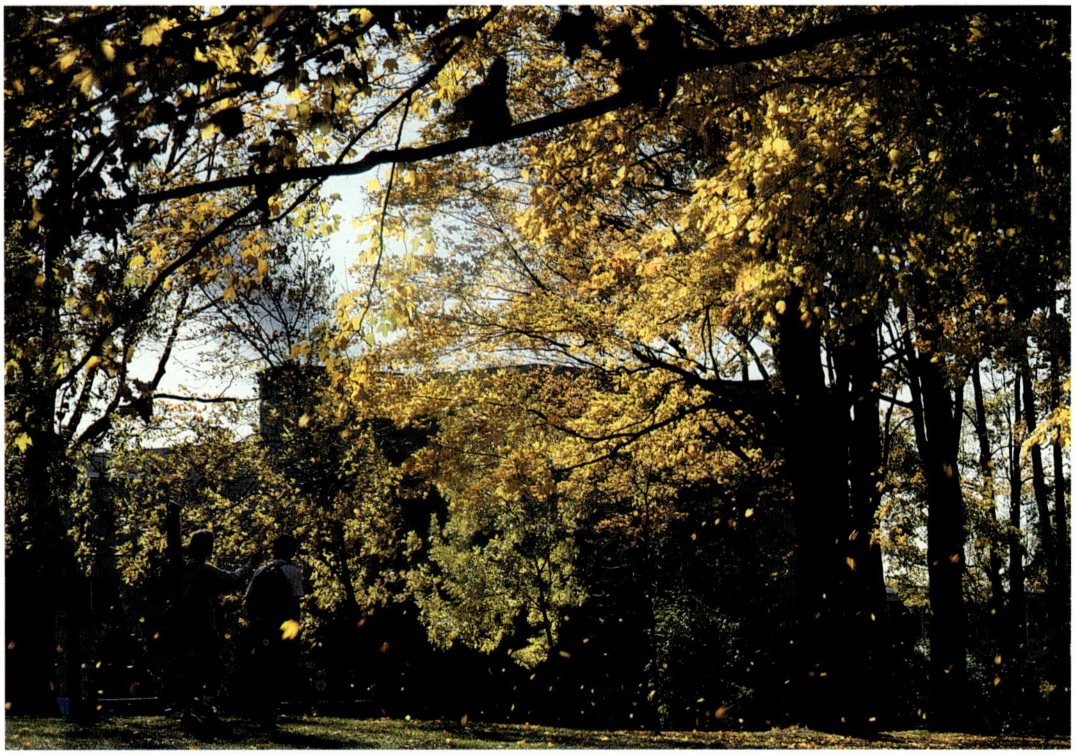

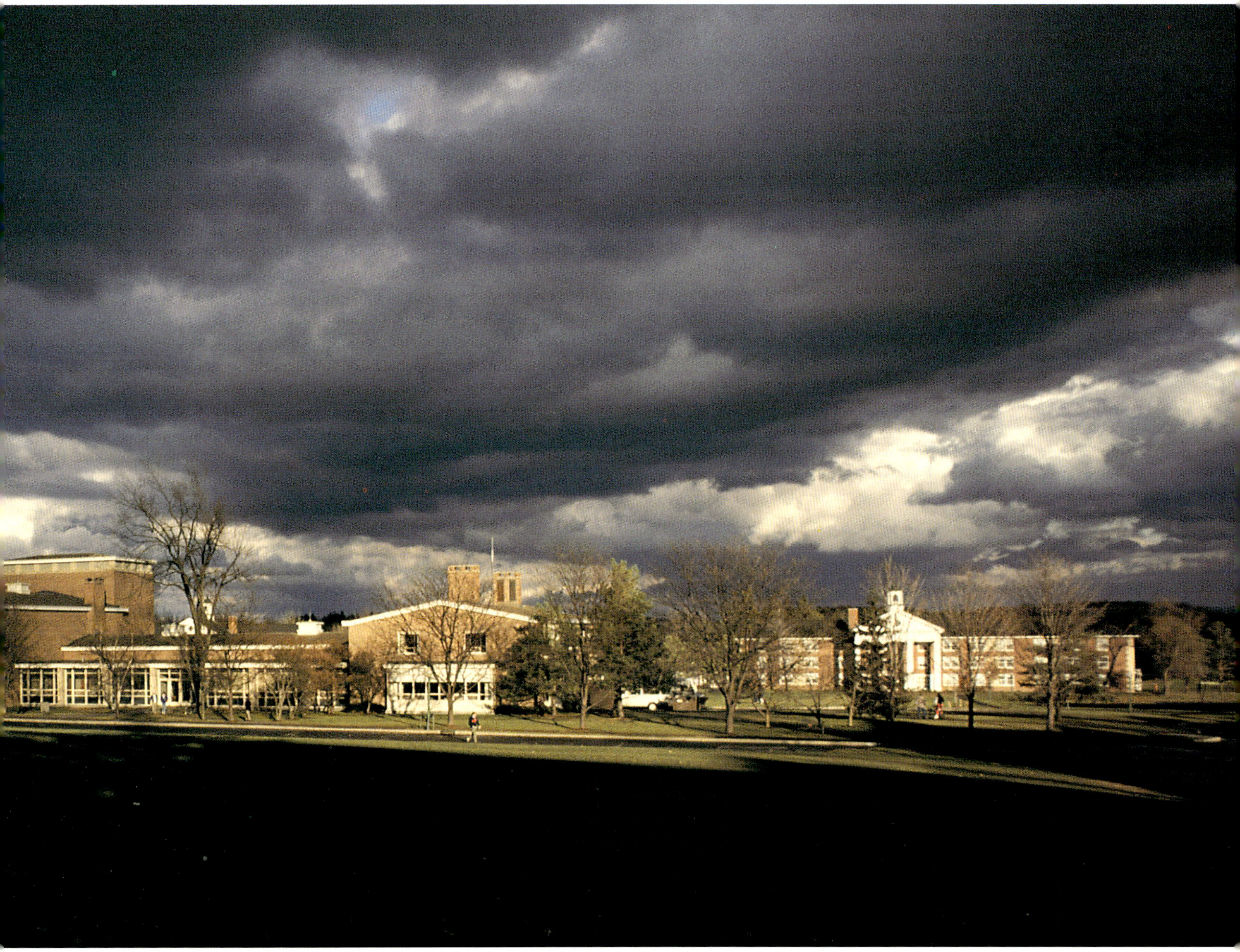

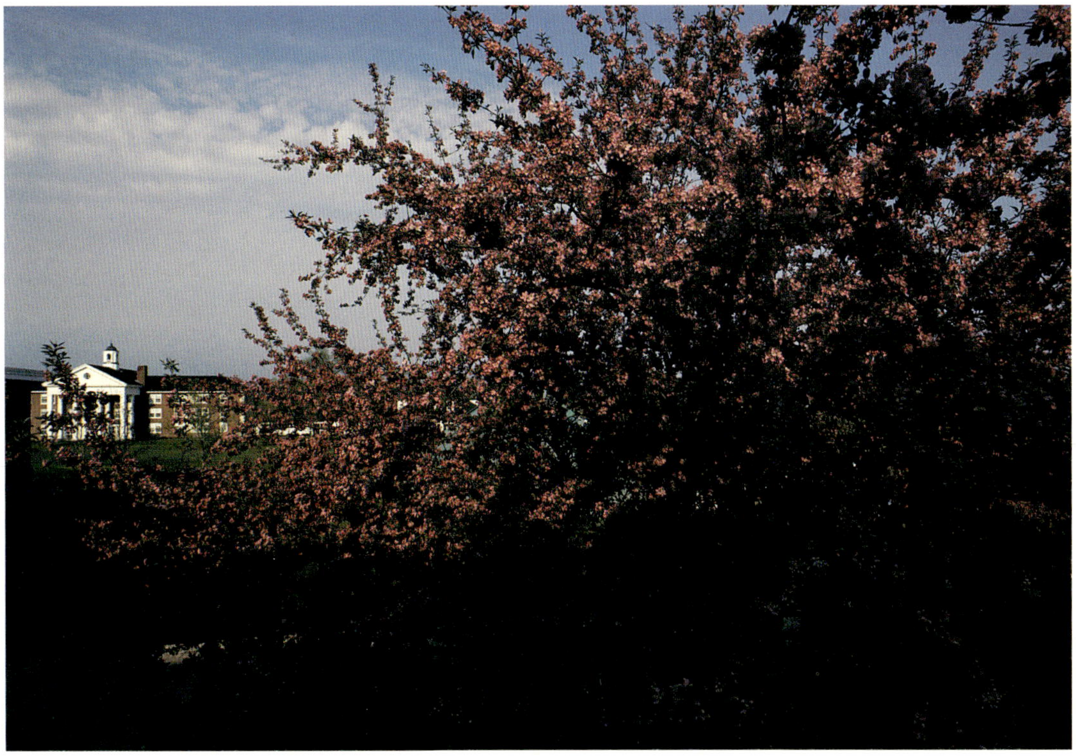

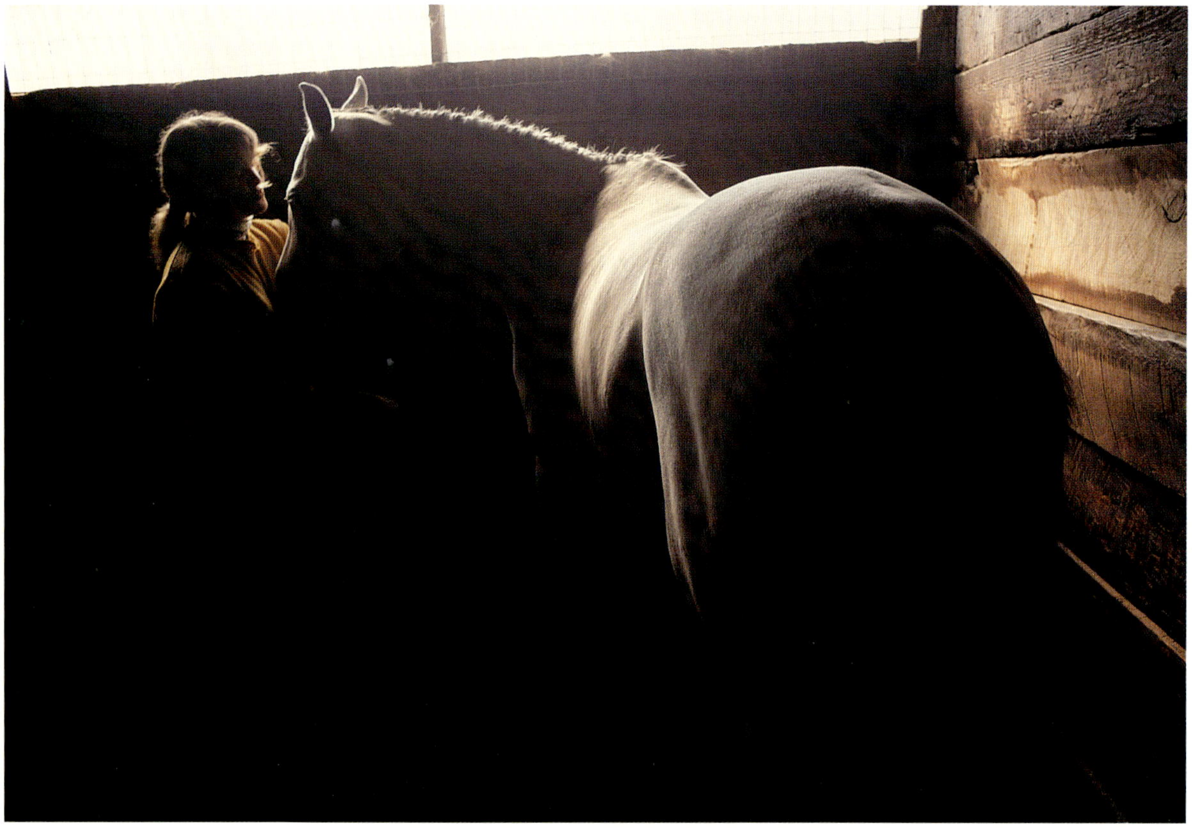

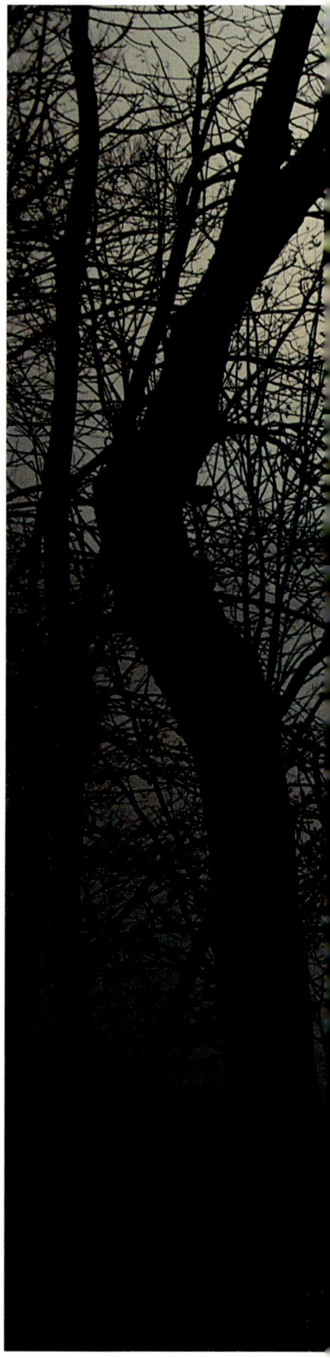

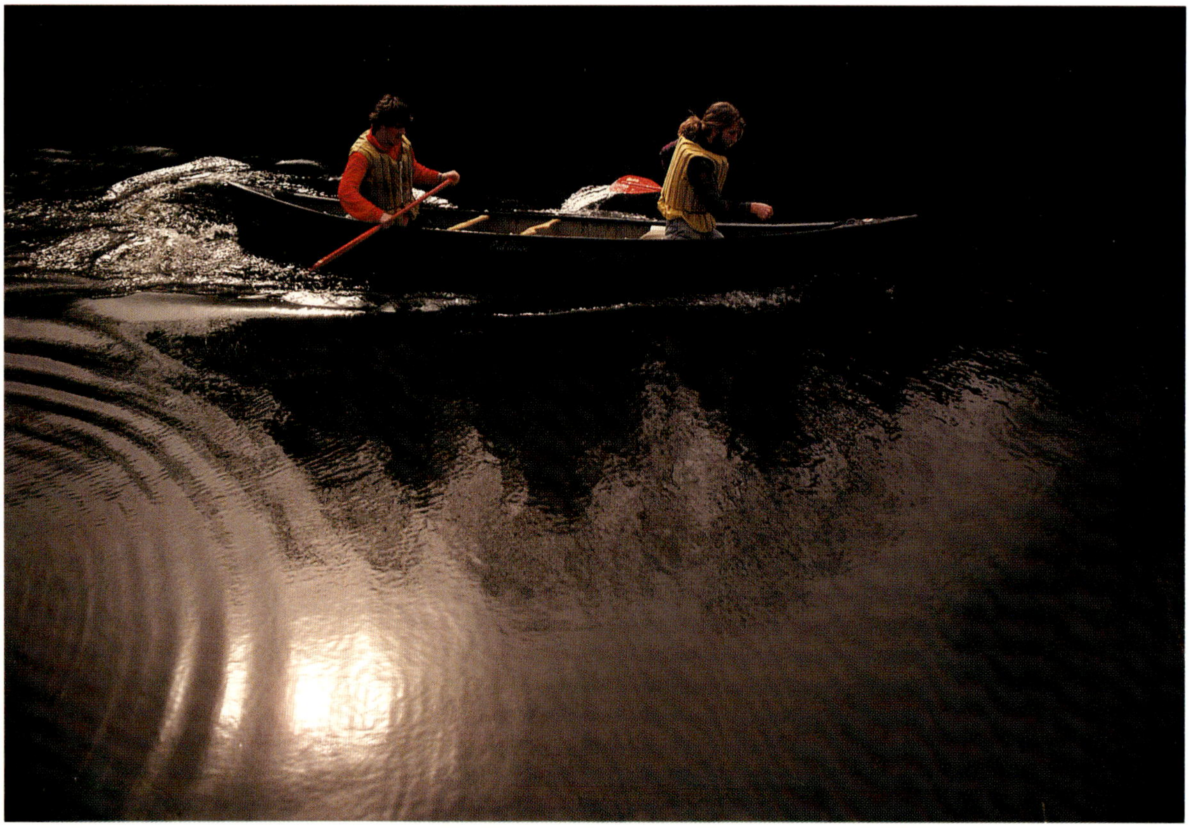

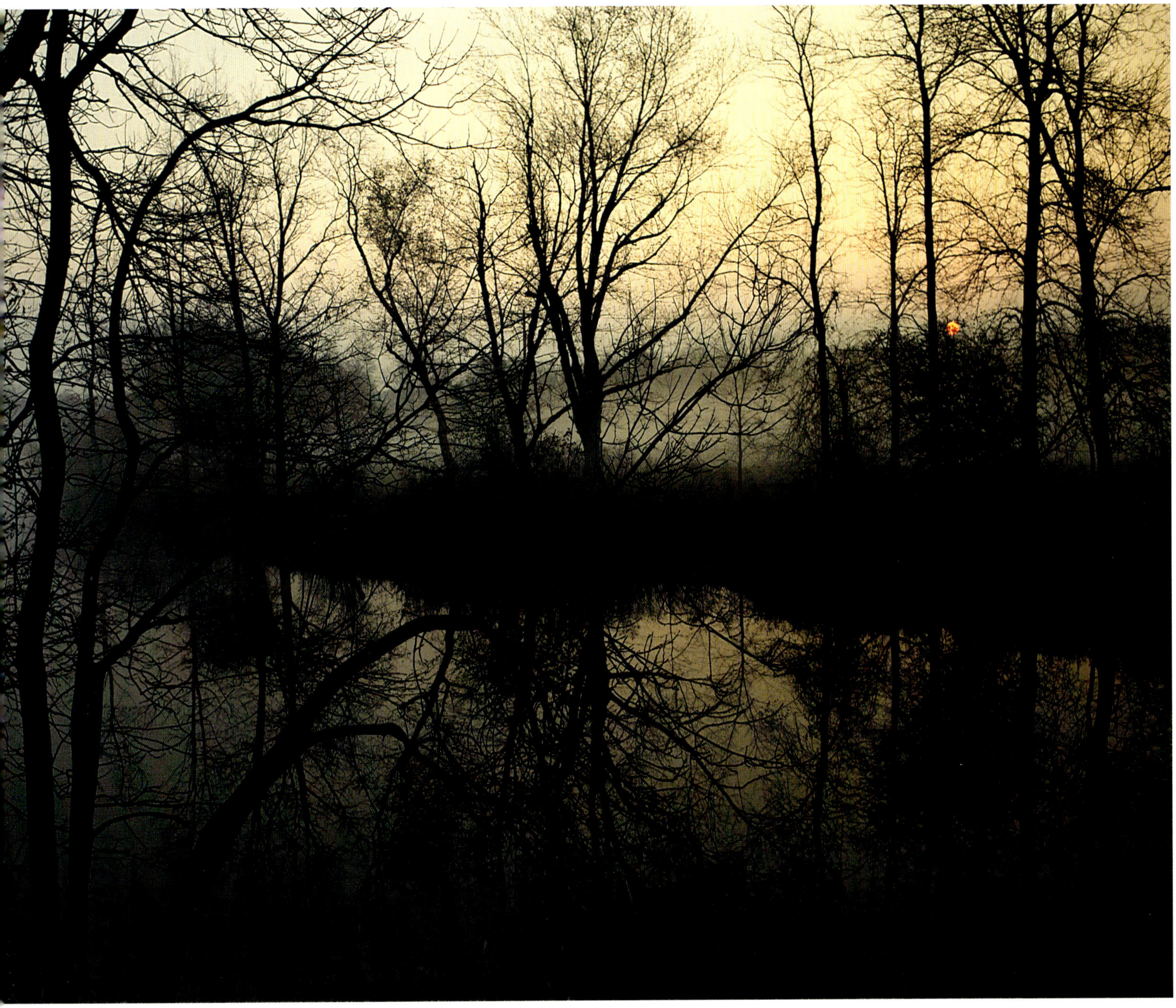

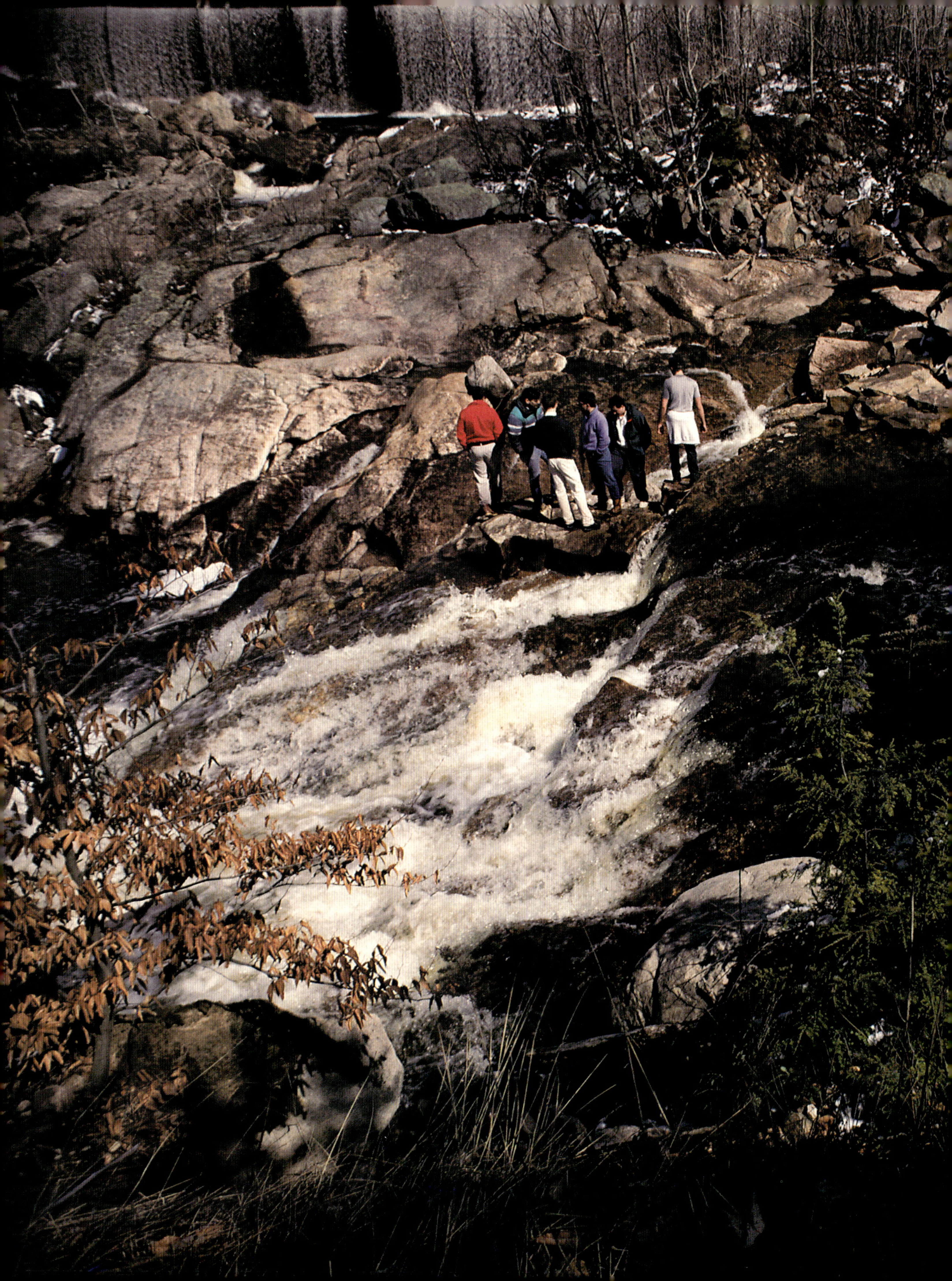

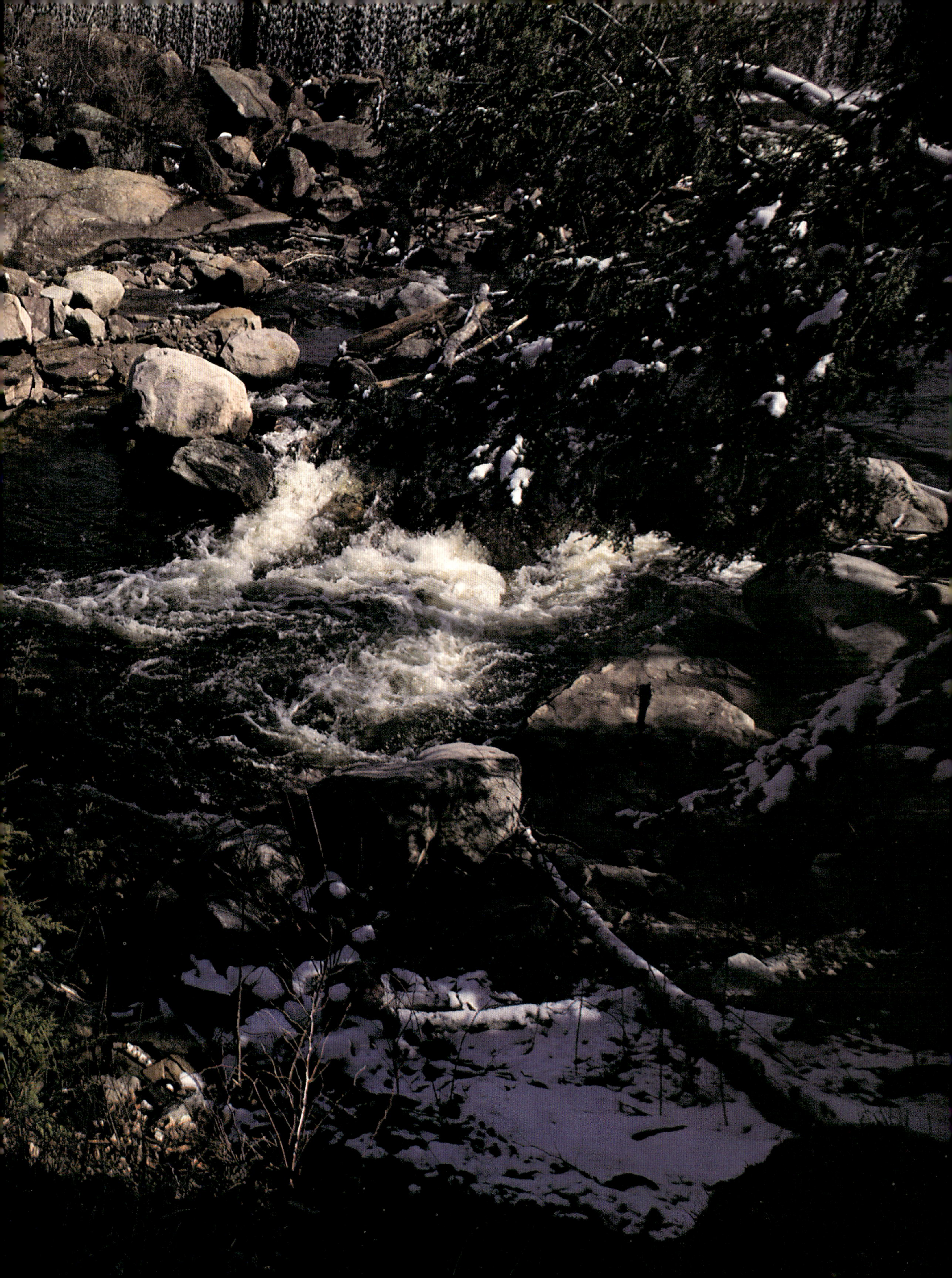

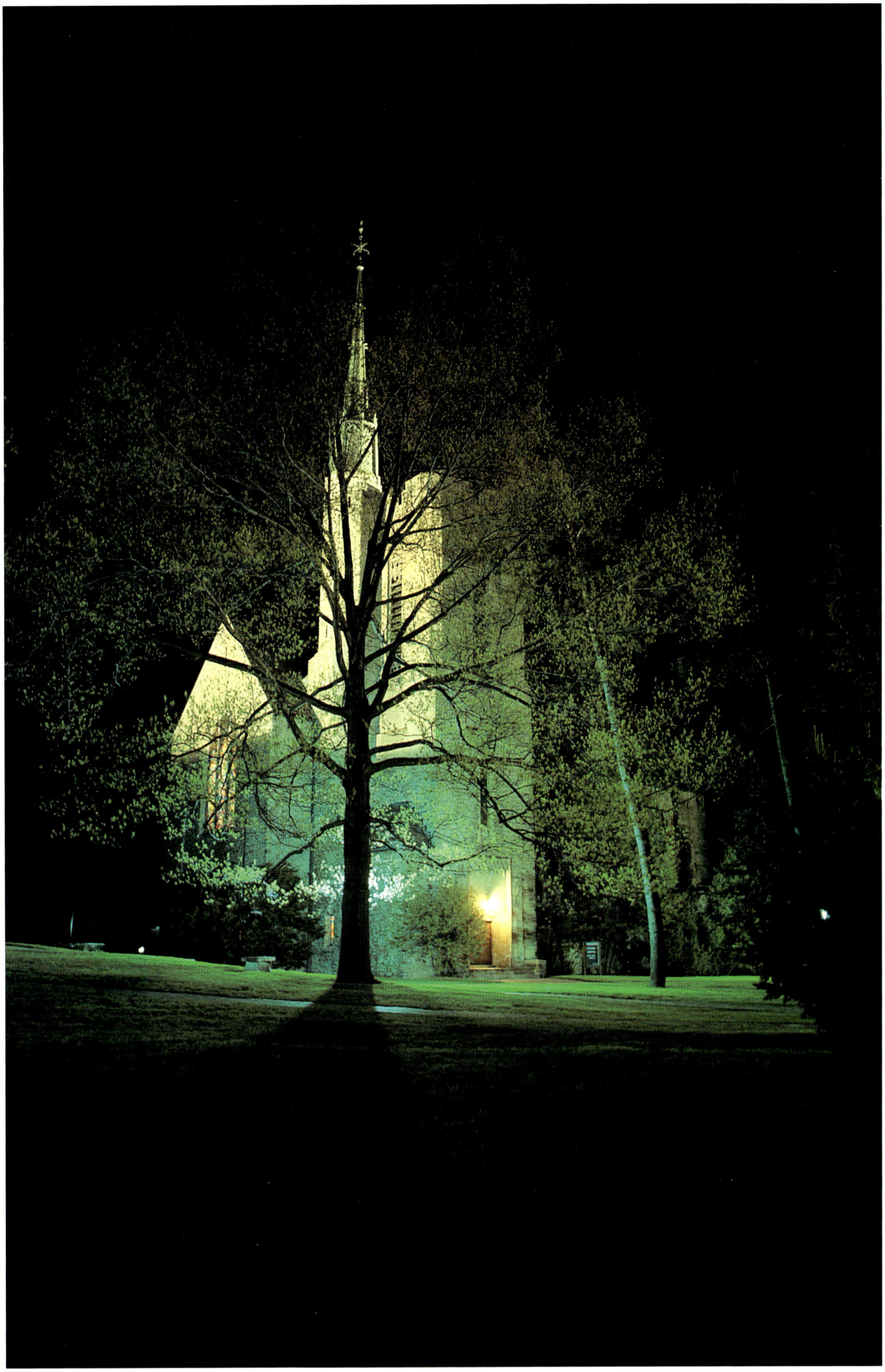

Of all the places where men work together, where their lives are constantly stimulated by the fresh possibilities that youth presents, a college should be an example of the spirit that makes men work effectively and happily. I deeply hope we may together achieve it here.

President Eugene Garrett Bewkes

E. J. Noble University Center

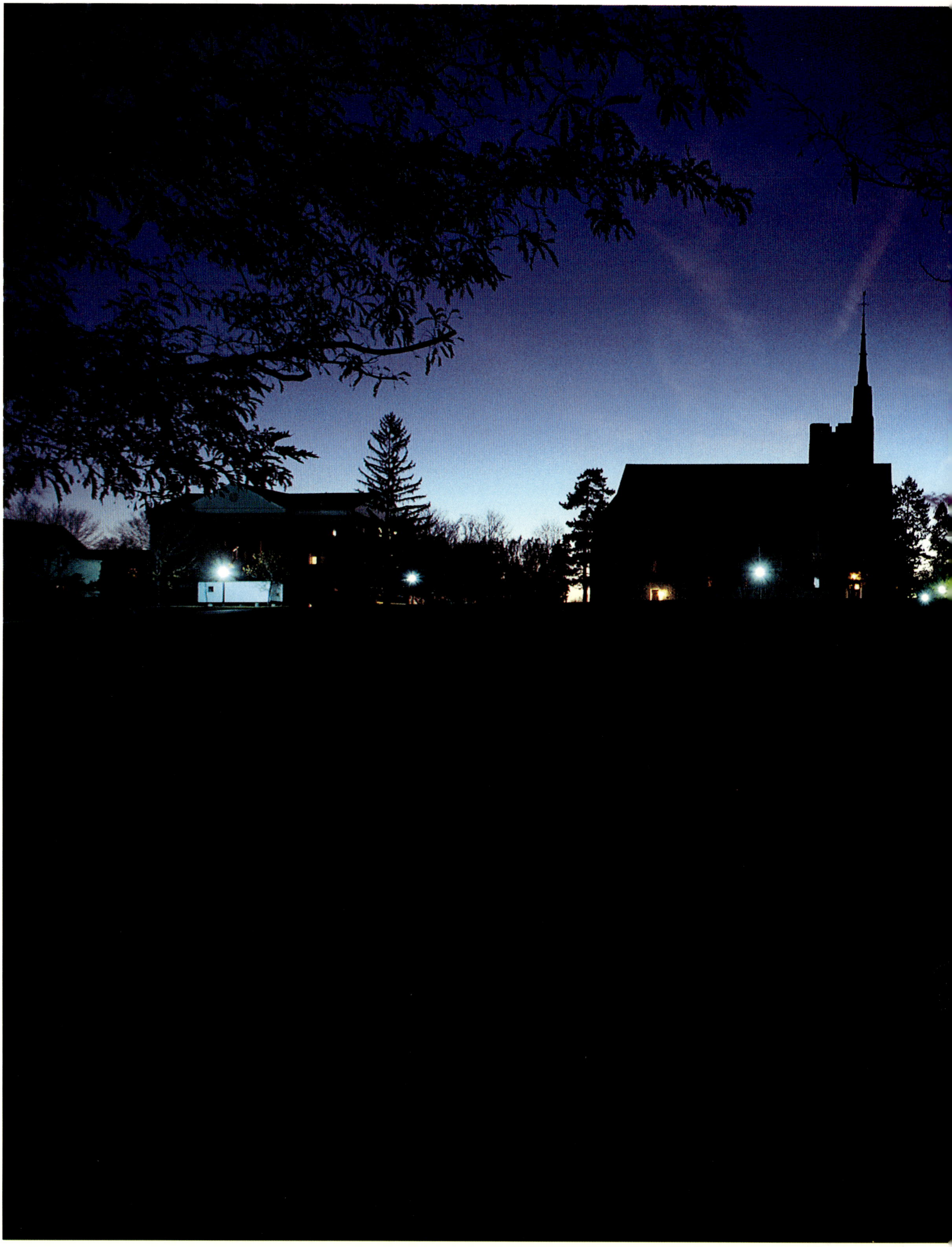

*Nestling 'neath the purple shadows
Of the Adirondack hills,
Lies our noble Alma Mater,
Thoughts of whom our mem'ry fills.
To her we bow in rev'rence
As we lay our tribute down
Before our dear St. Lawrence,
'Neath the Scarlet and the Brown.*

From "A Tribute"

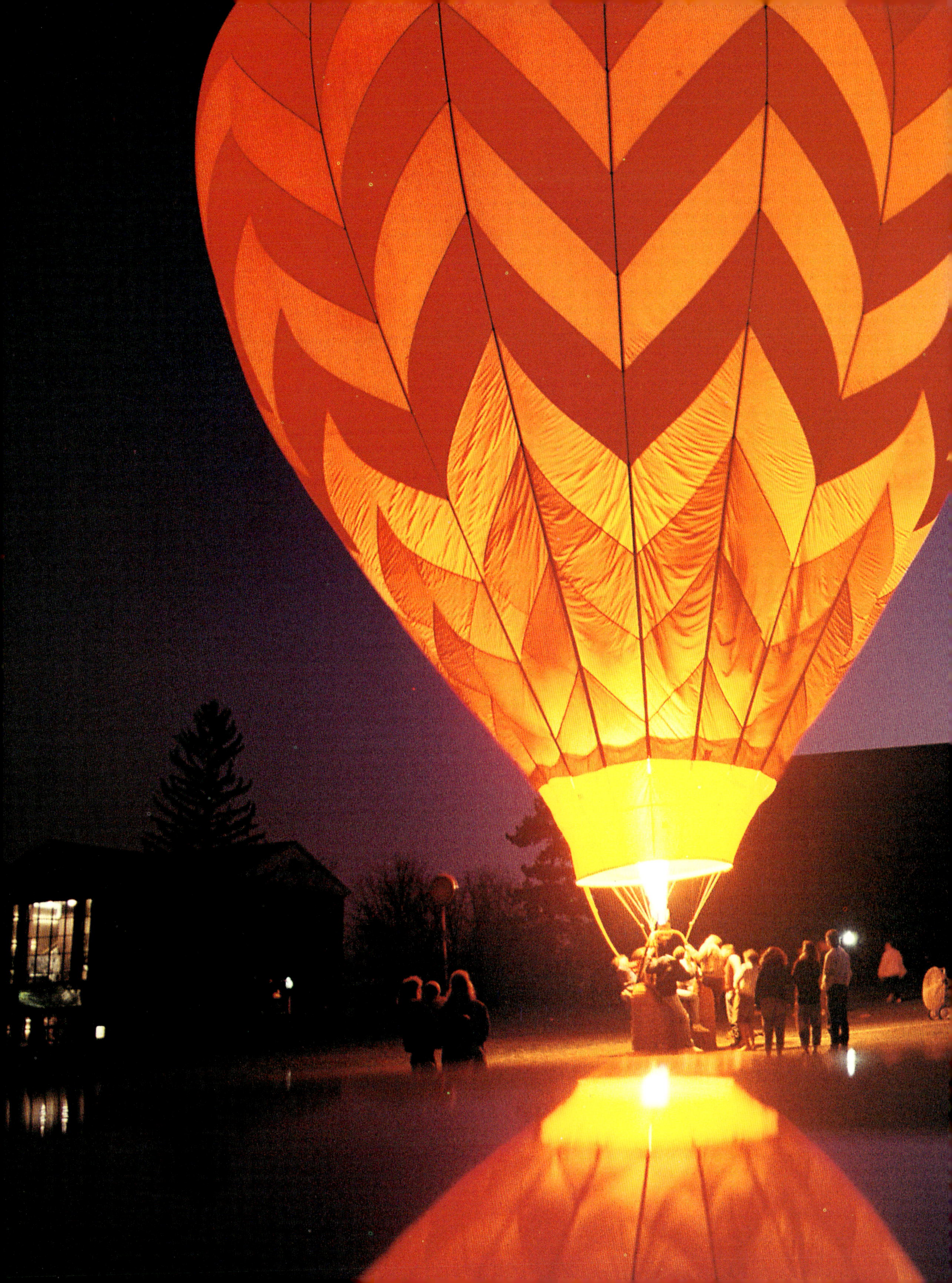

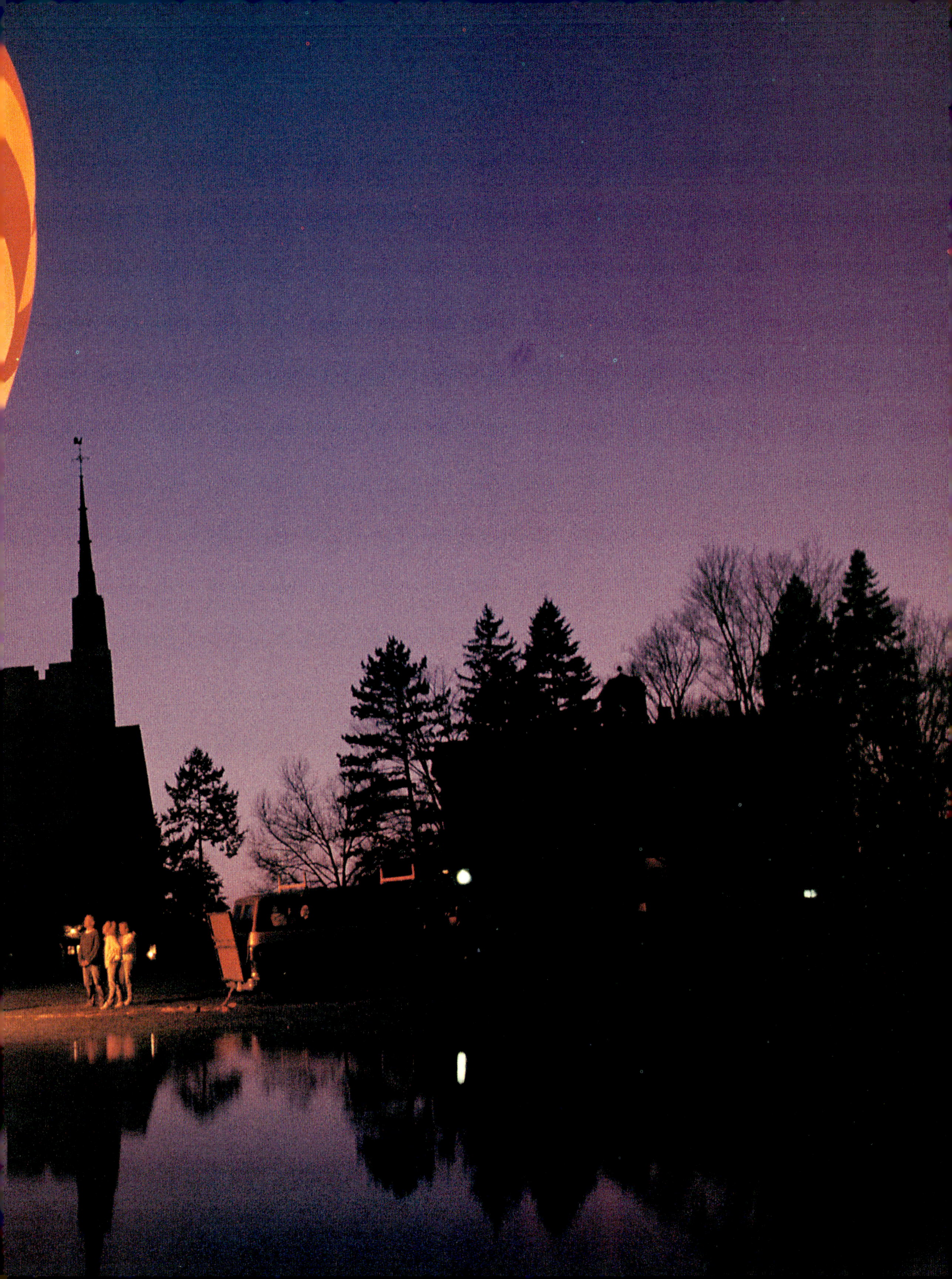

St. Lawrence University turns out balanced, intelligent, competent people with a sense of purpose, a humaneness, and a great deal of integrity. A big part of our reward is associating with these young people.

Alfred C. Viebranz '42 Chairman of the Board of Trustees, 1978

Parents Weekend

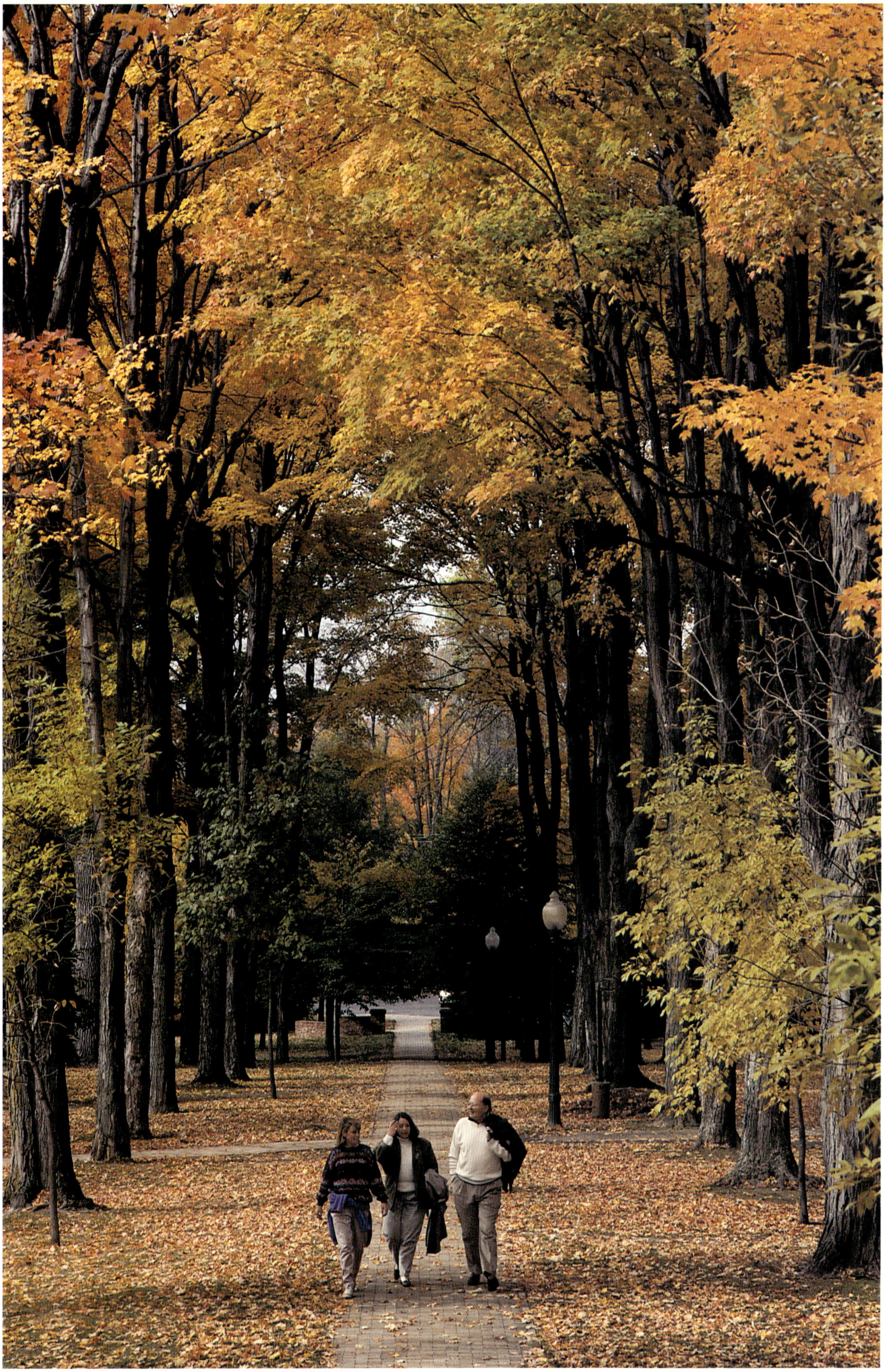

One coach once referred to St. Lawrence University and its athletic programs as "the little big time." He was referring both to SLU's athletic successes and the facilities and atmosphere which surround SLU athletes. Saint athletes are winners — winners to an extent which would make most of the country's Division I schools envious.

Wally Johnson, Director of Sports Information, 1981

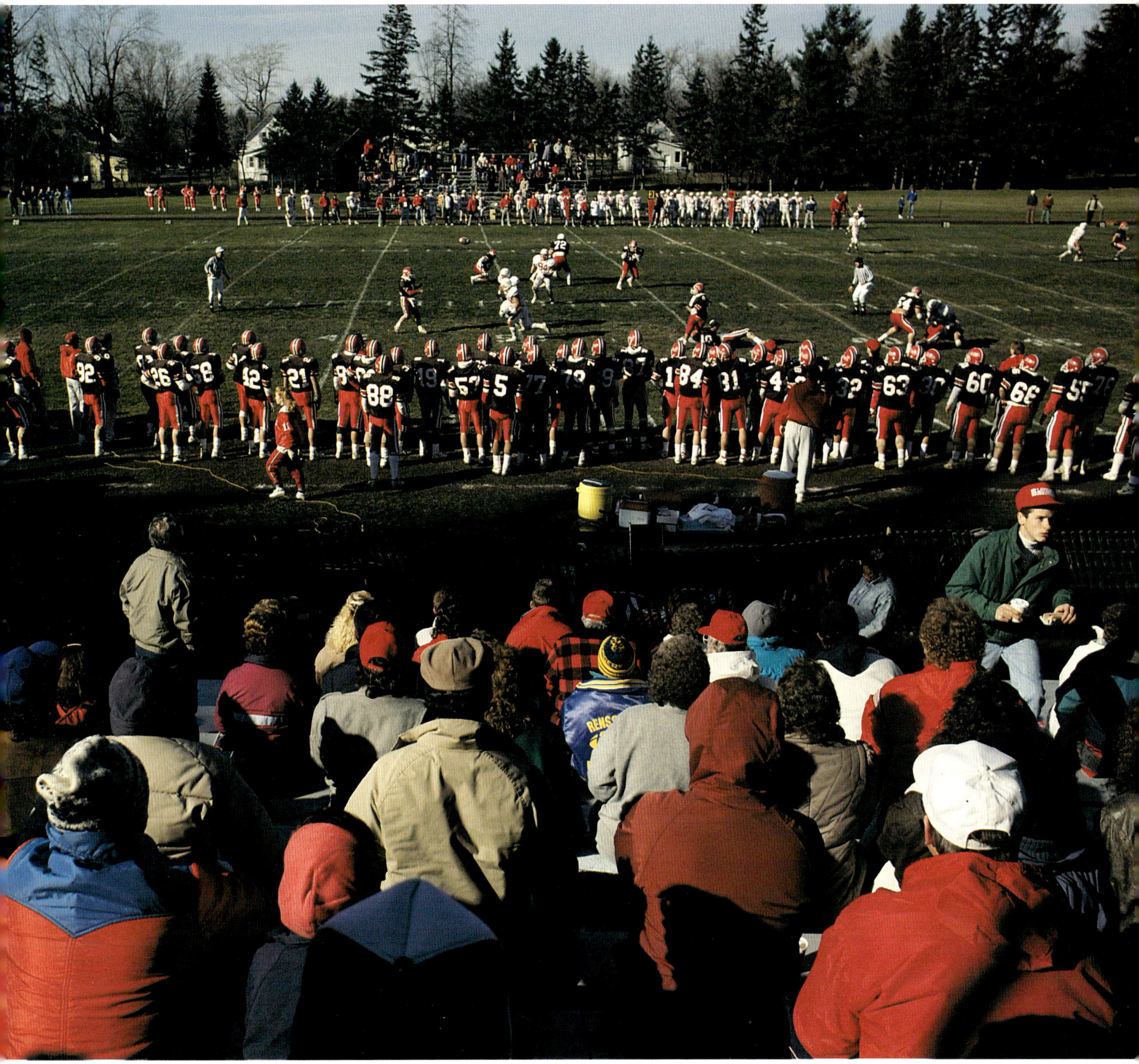

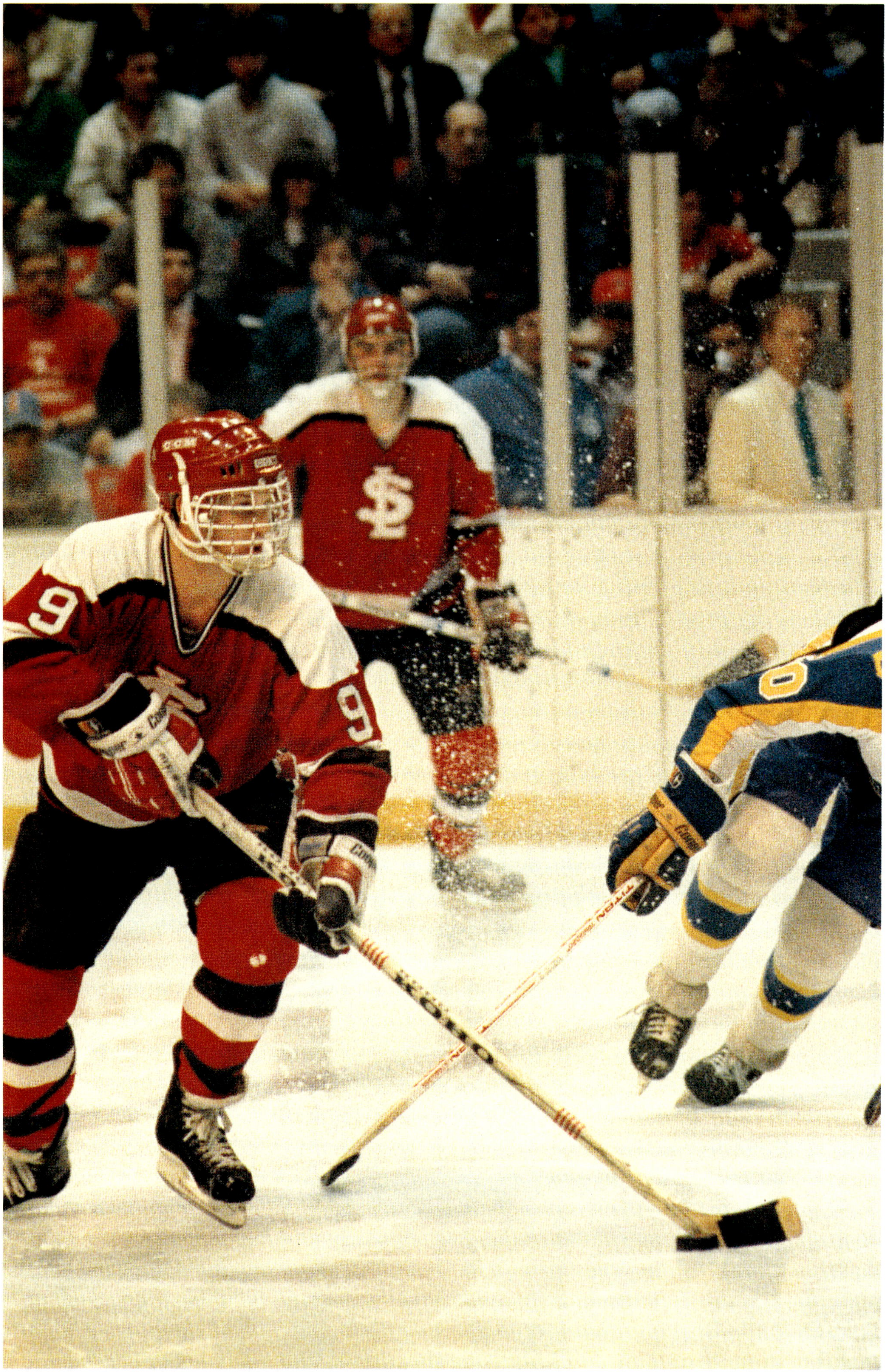
CCM
SL
KOHO

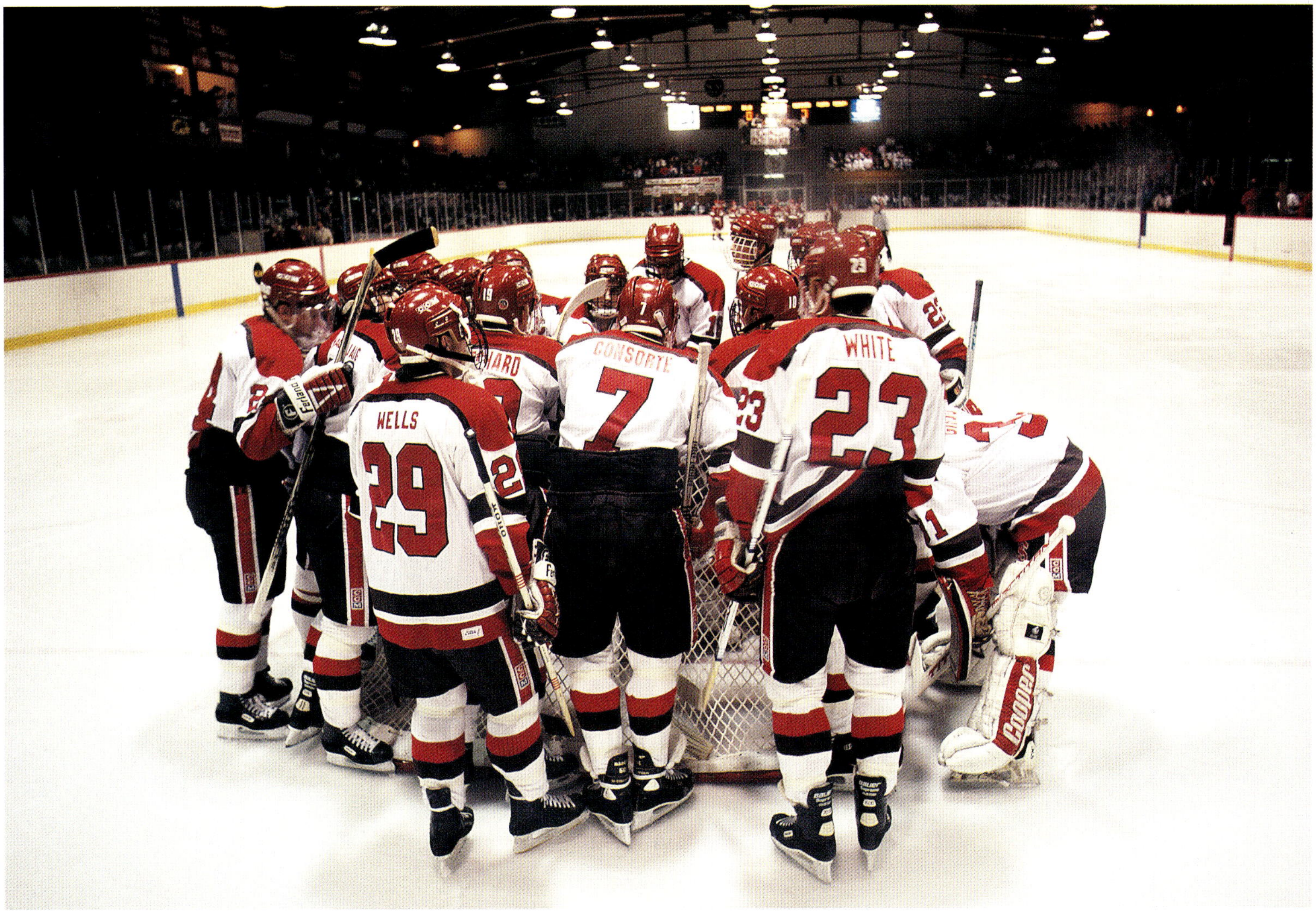
WELLS
29
CONSORTE
7
WHITE
23

60

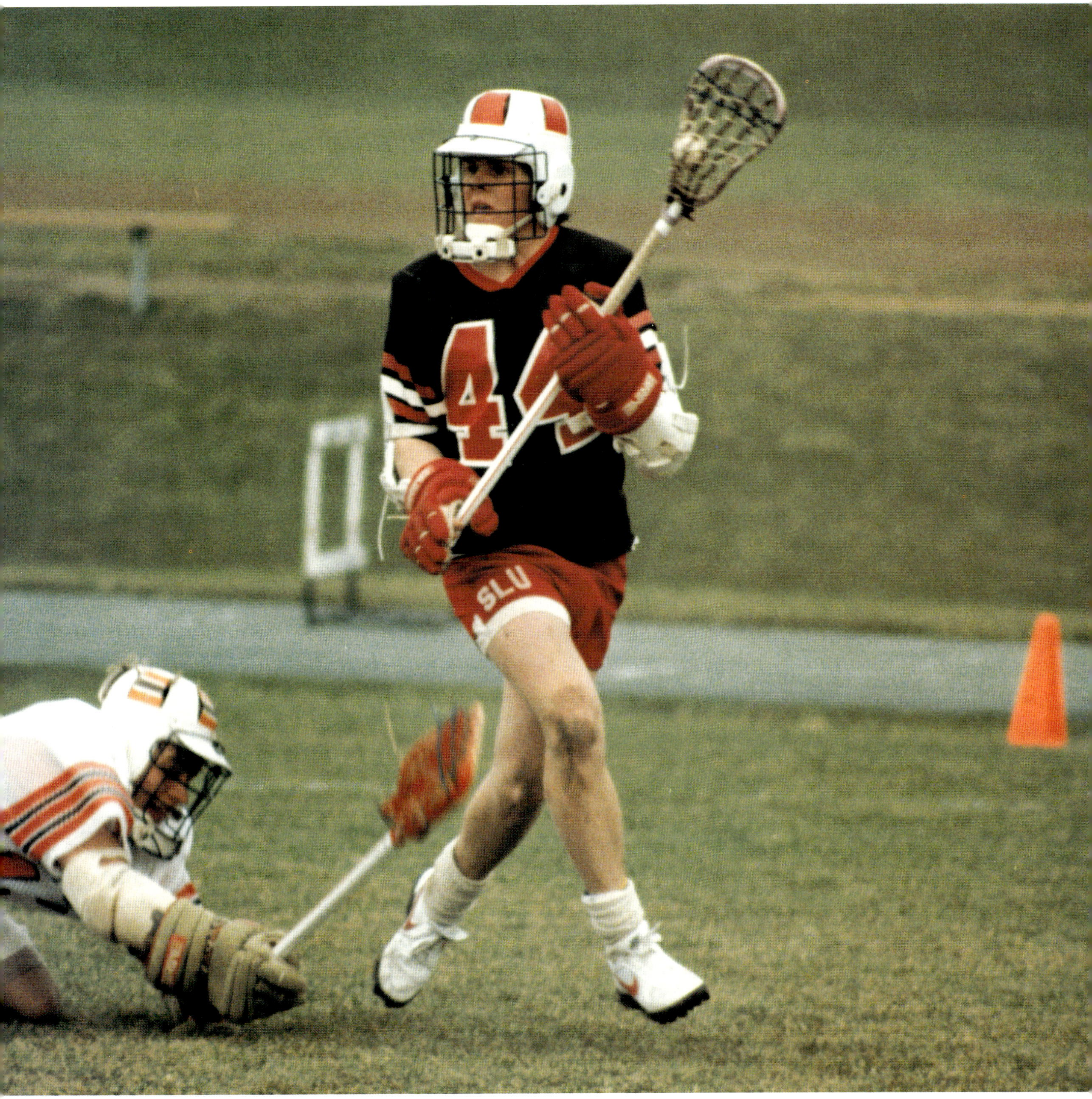
SLU

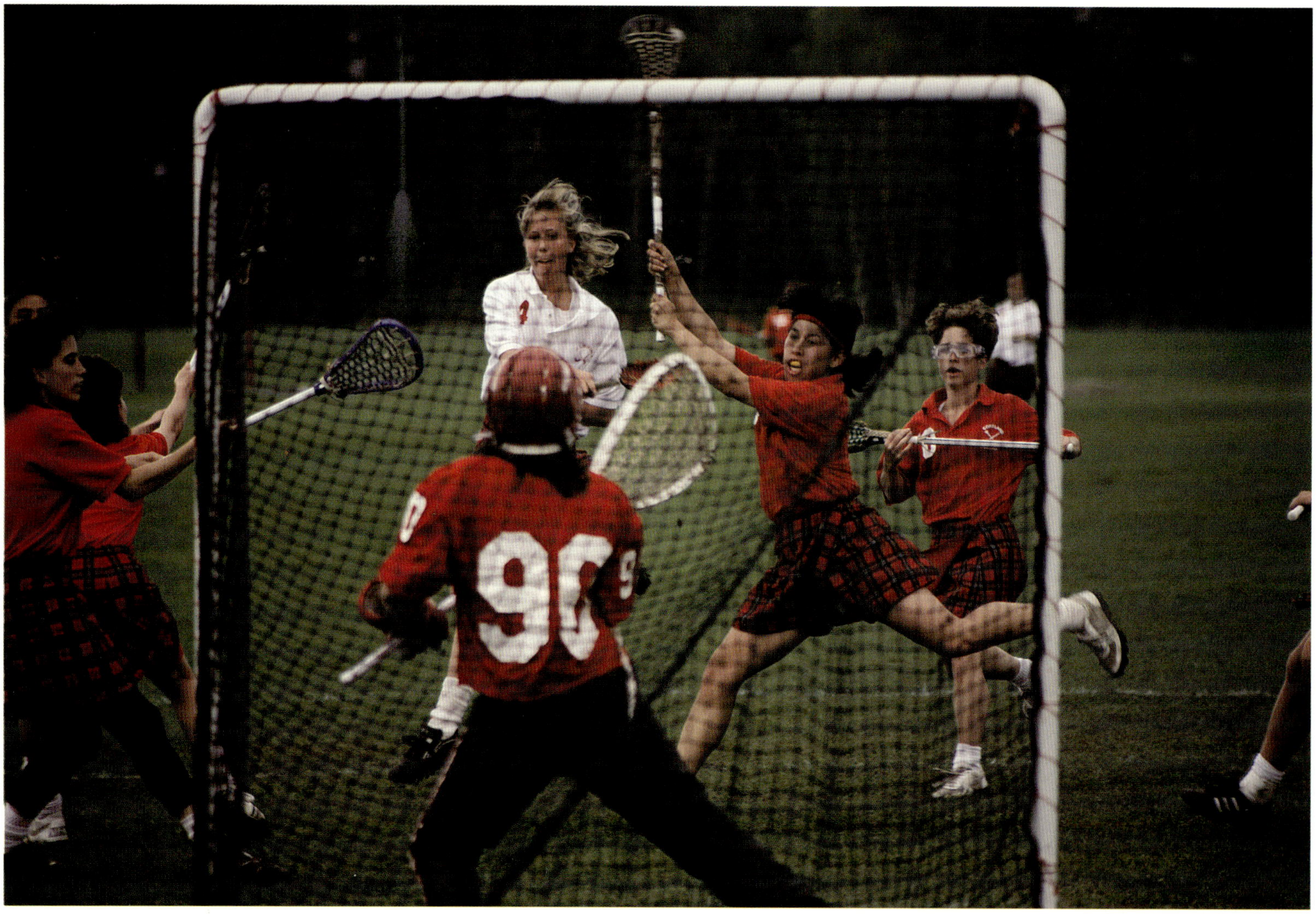
90

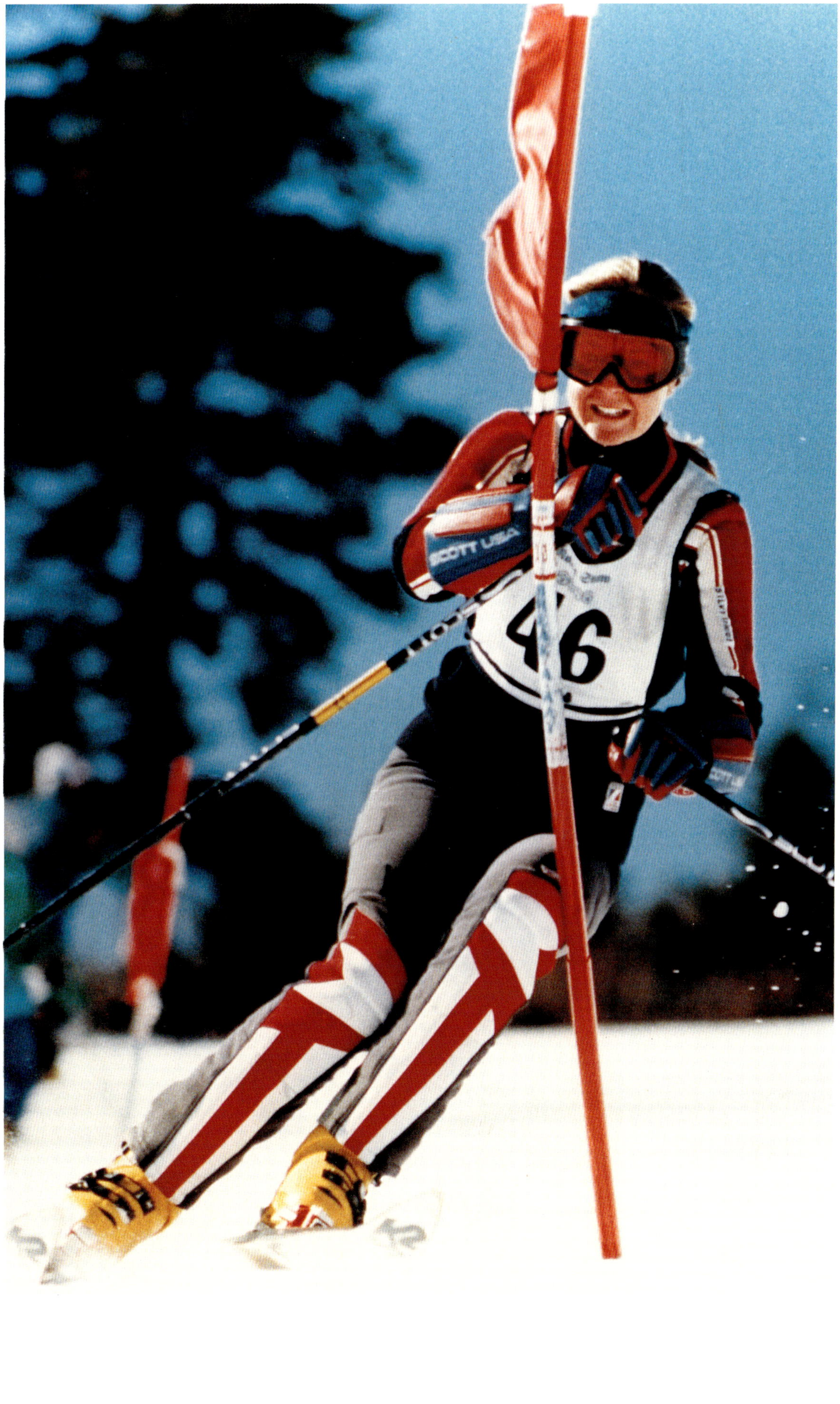
SCOTT USA
46

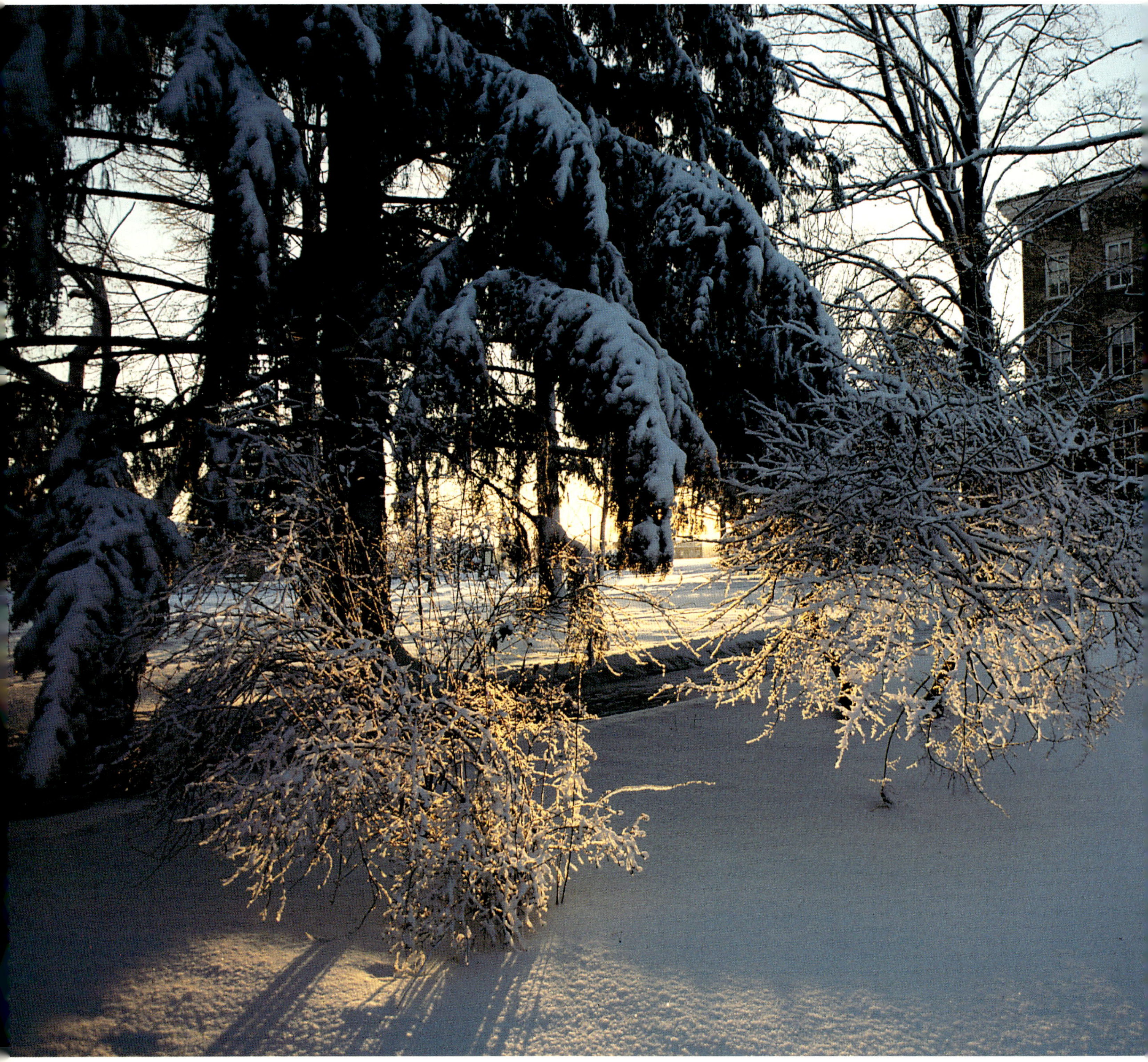

65

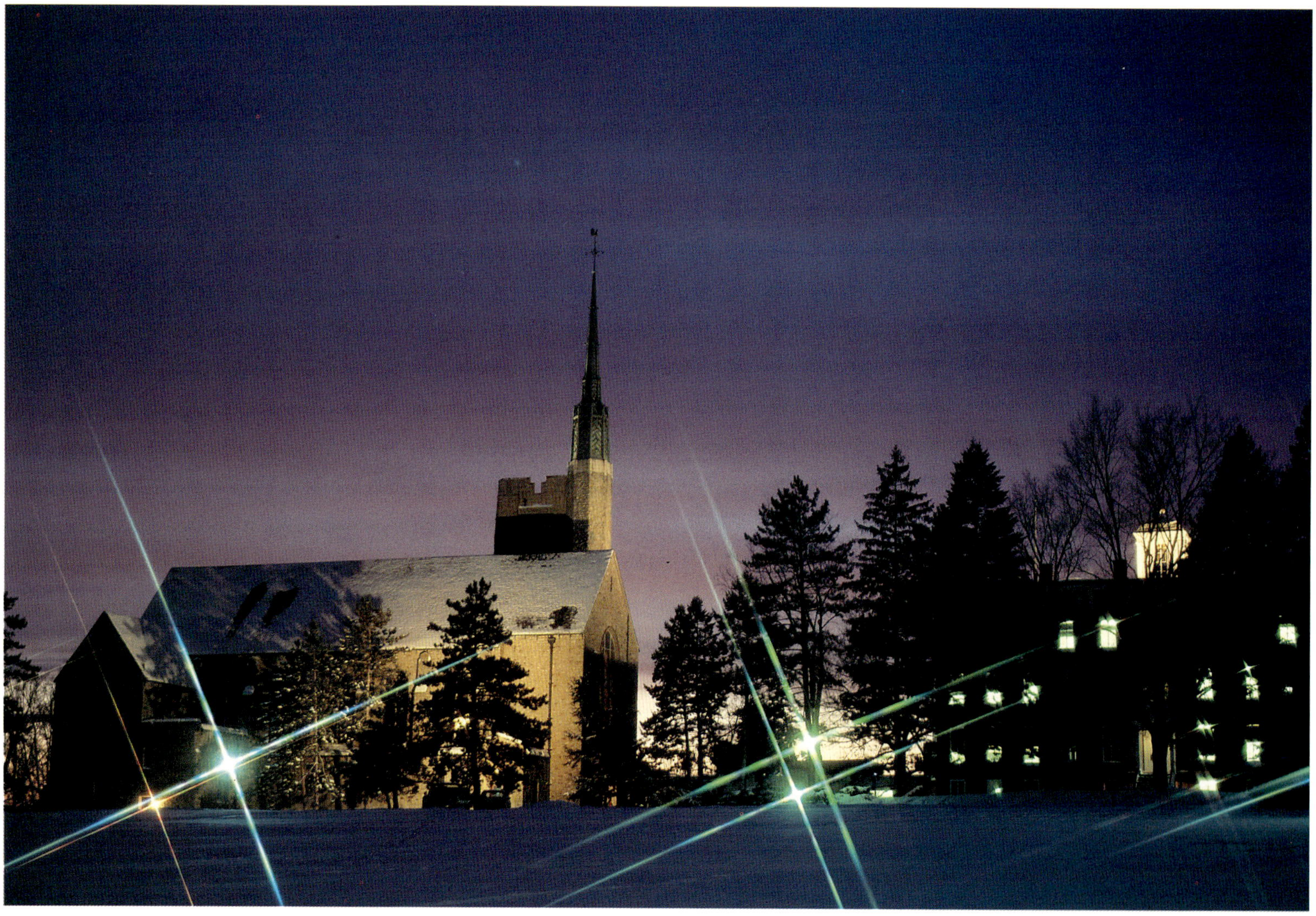

Candlelight Ceremony of Lessons and Carols

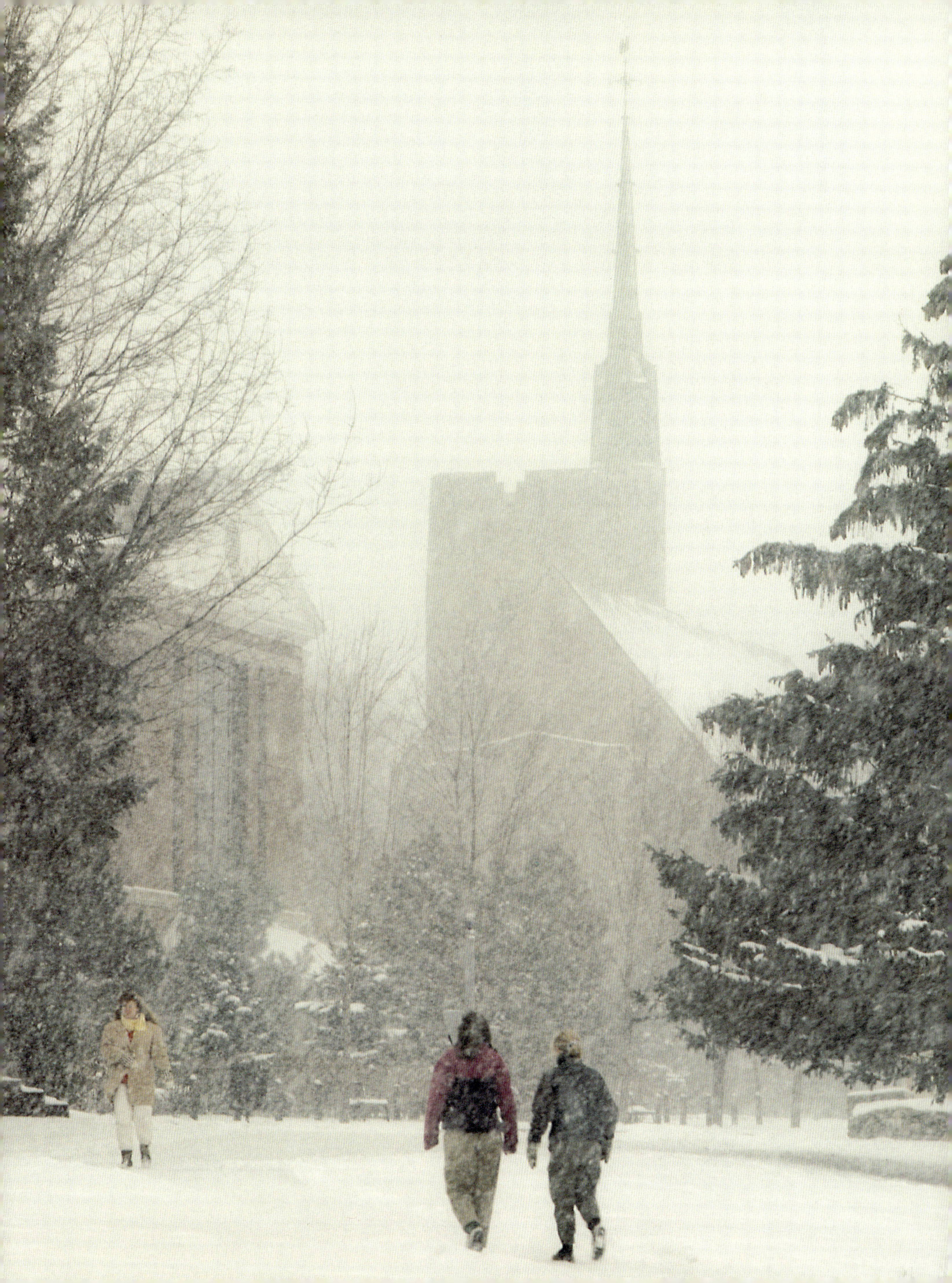

The Laurentian Singers

Students are not essentially different from students of an earlier, slower-paced time. They tend to be the same mixture of good sense and occasional bad judgement, they have the same refreshing likableness.

President Eugene Garrett Bewkes, in the April, 1963 *Bulletin*

72

73

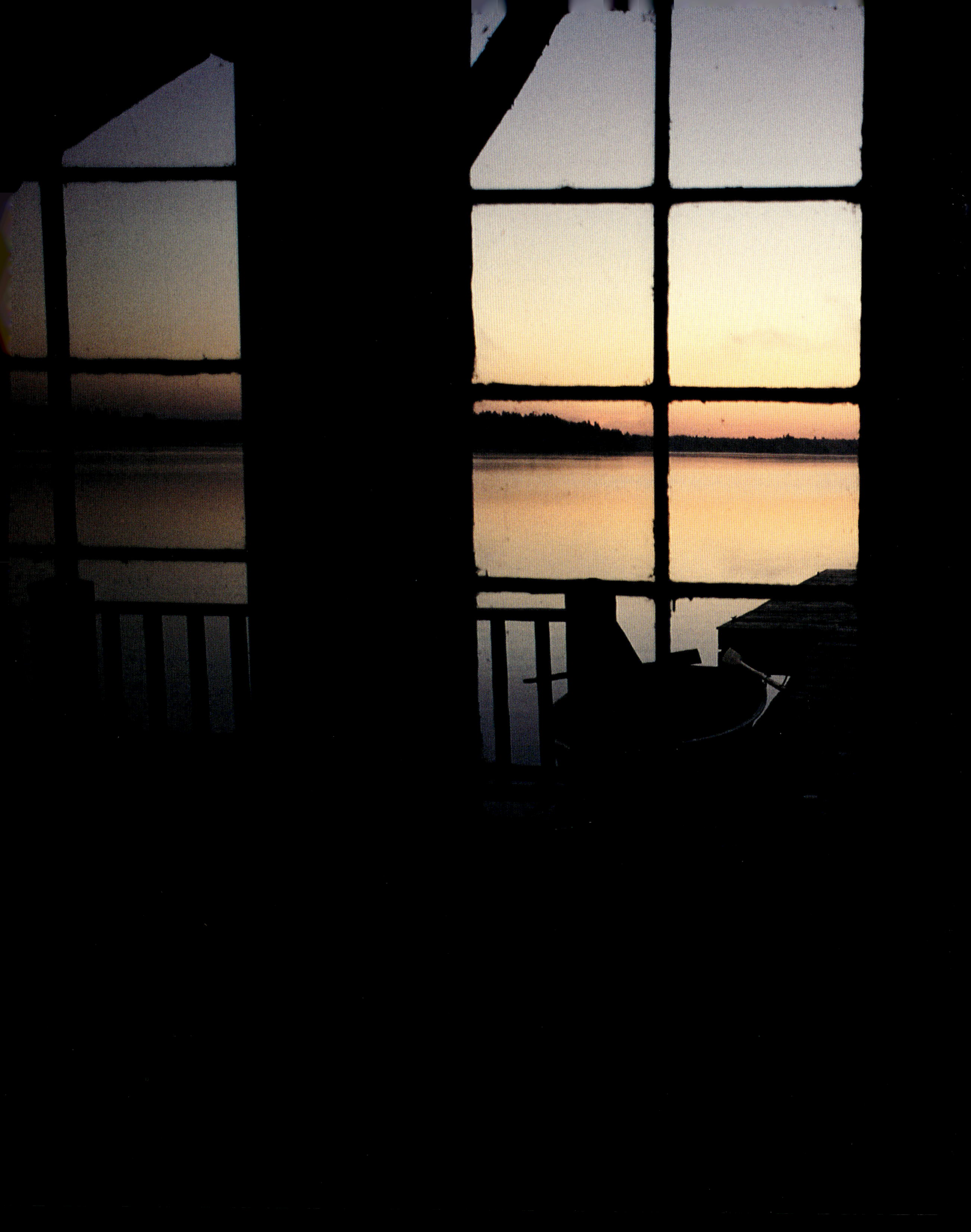

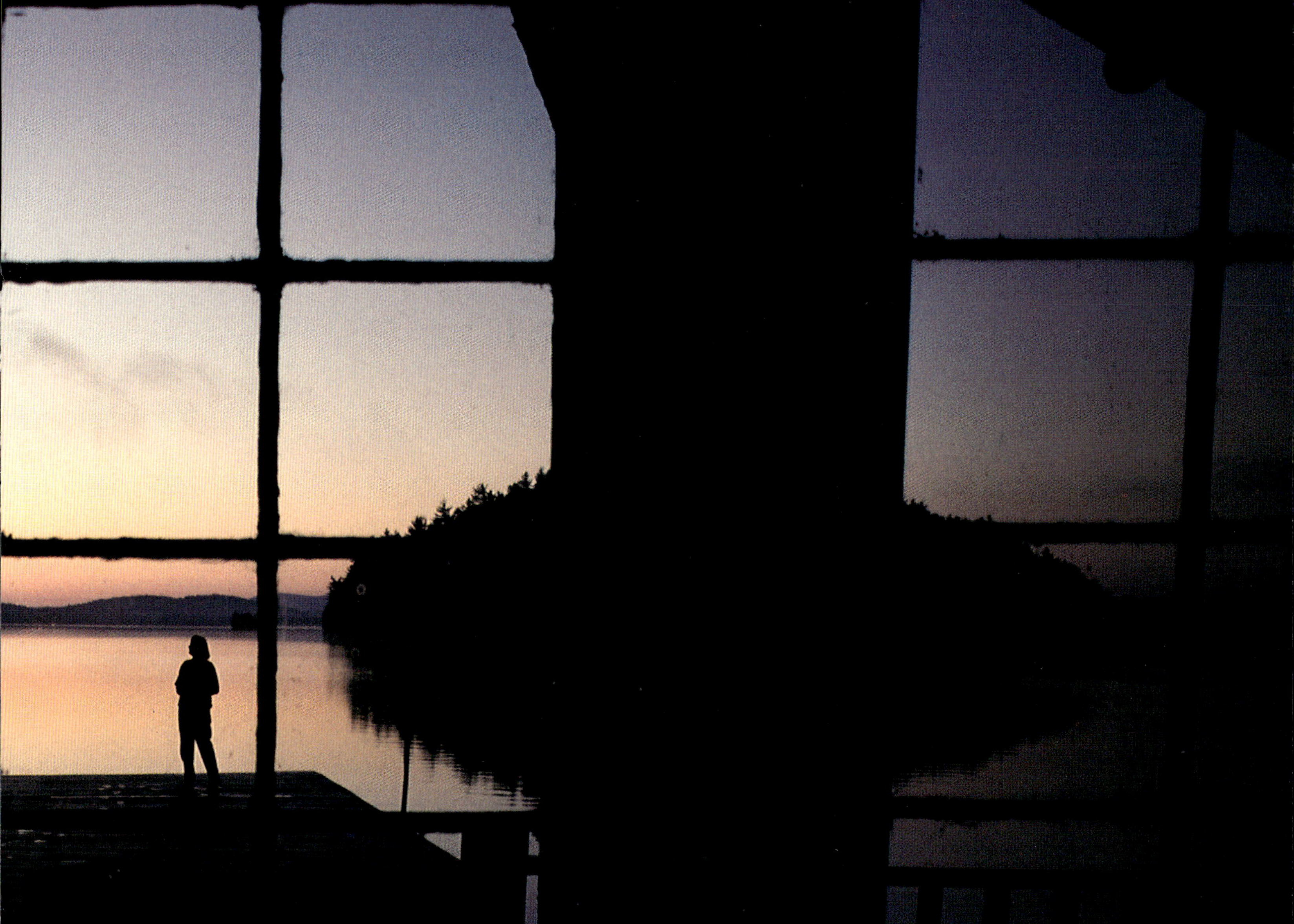

Catamount Lodge

Canaras Conference Center

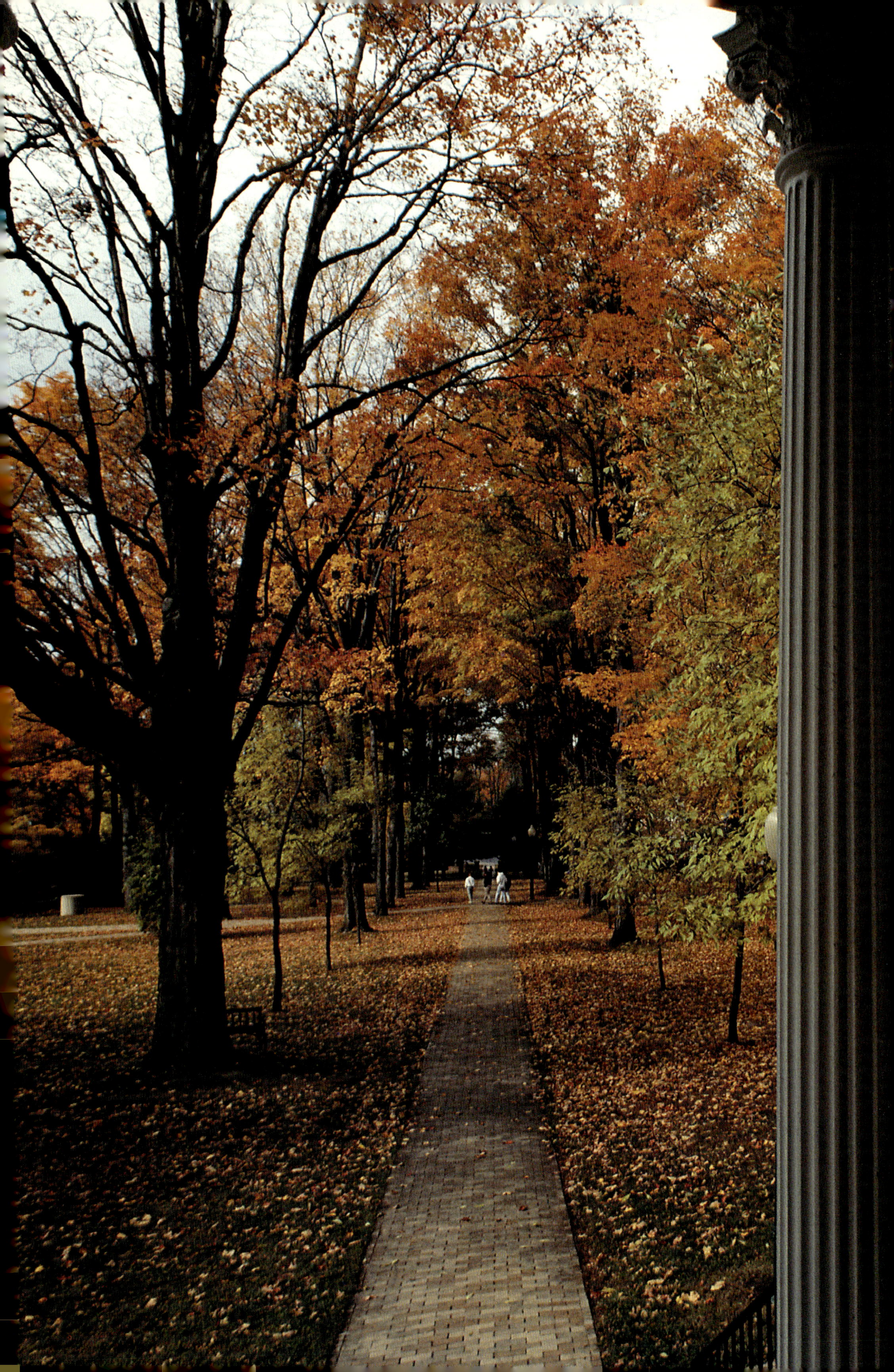

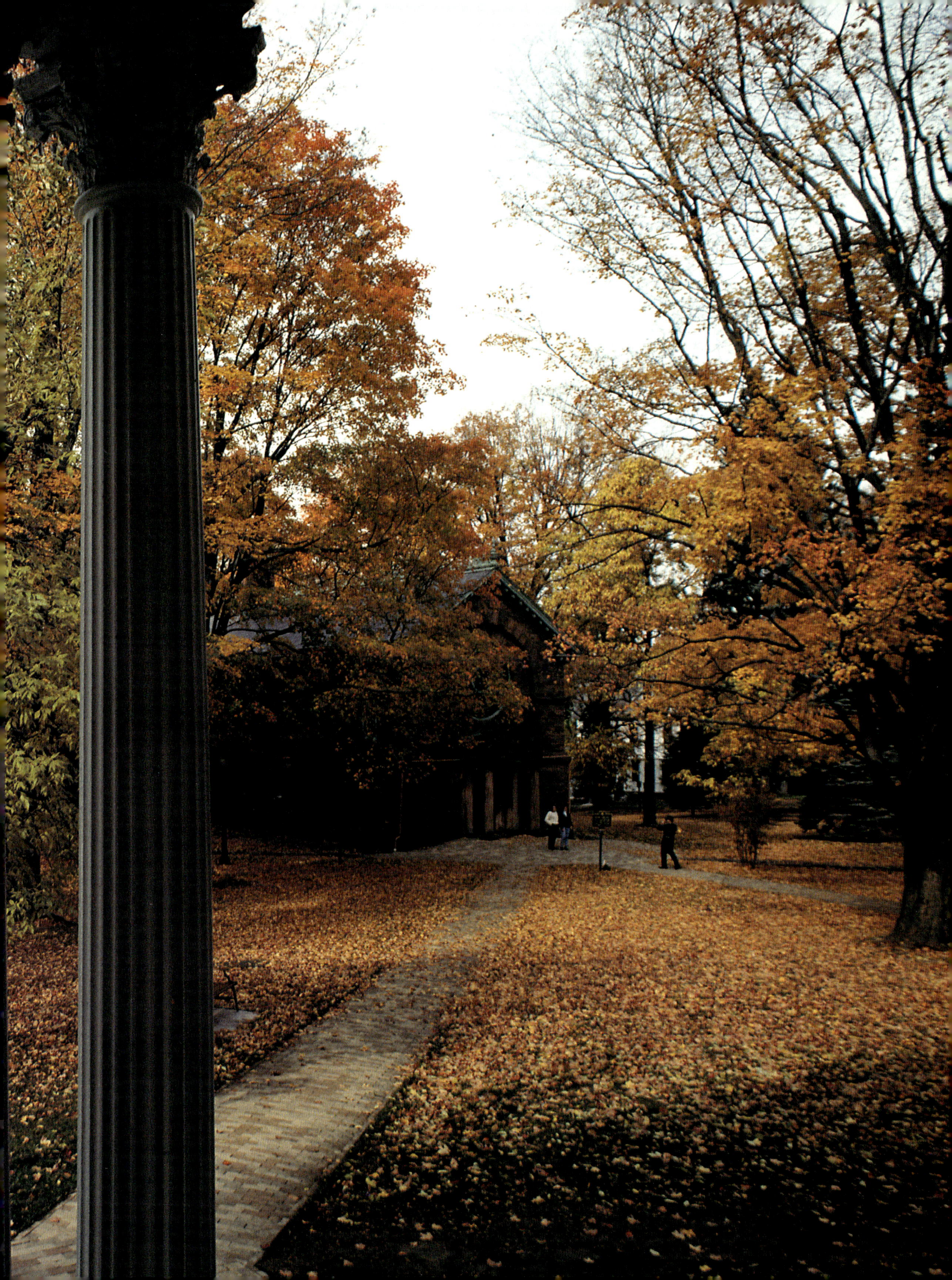

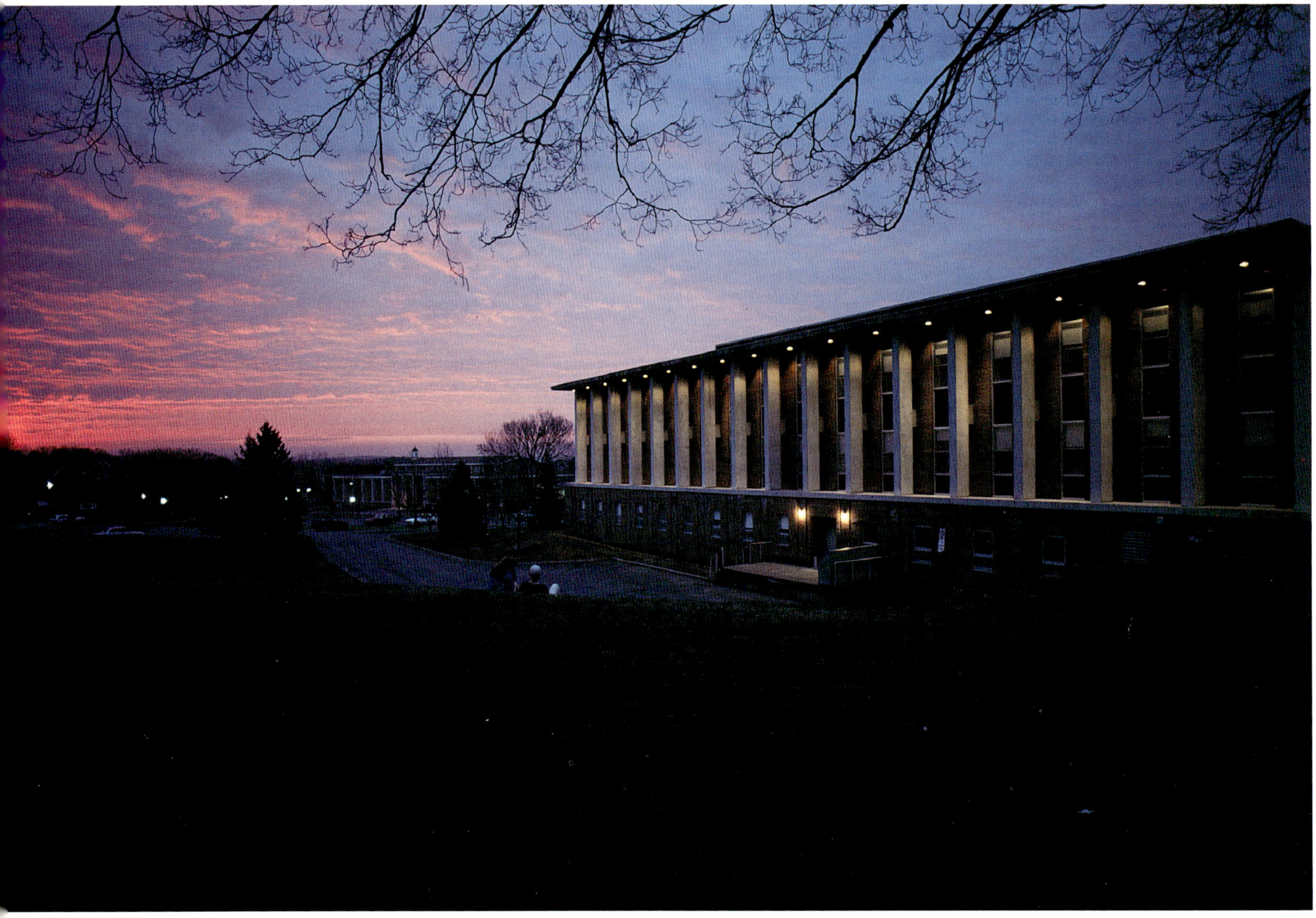

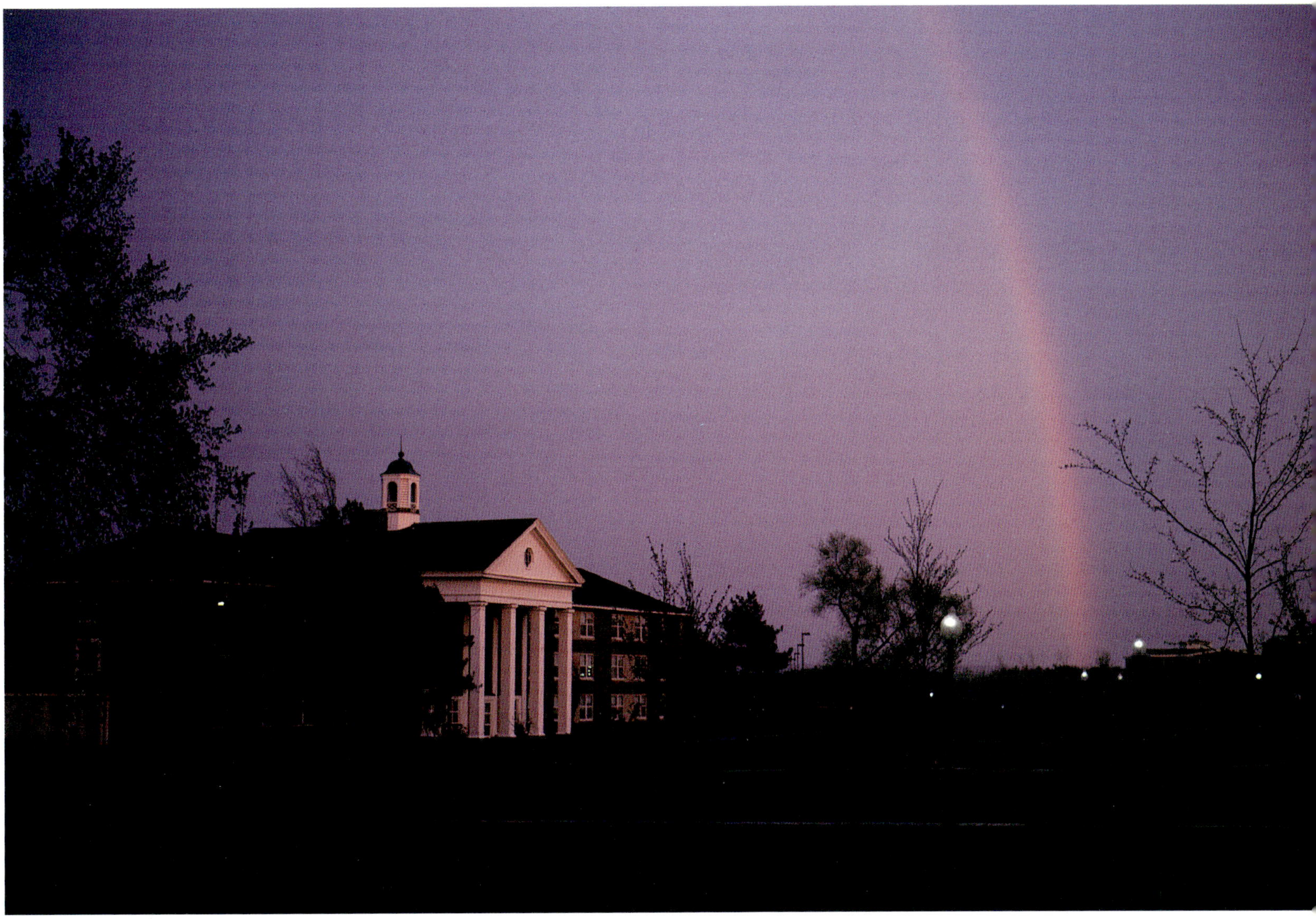

Herring-Cole Hall

We are fortunate to have the Griffiths Arts Center, a going concern we conceive of as an essential part of the University's educational program. It ranks with the library and the science center, the classroom and the studies as a basic channel through which our objectives are achieved.

President Frank Piskor, at university convocation, September 24, 1969.

84

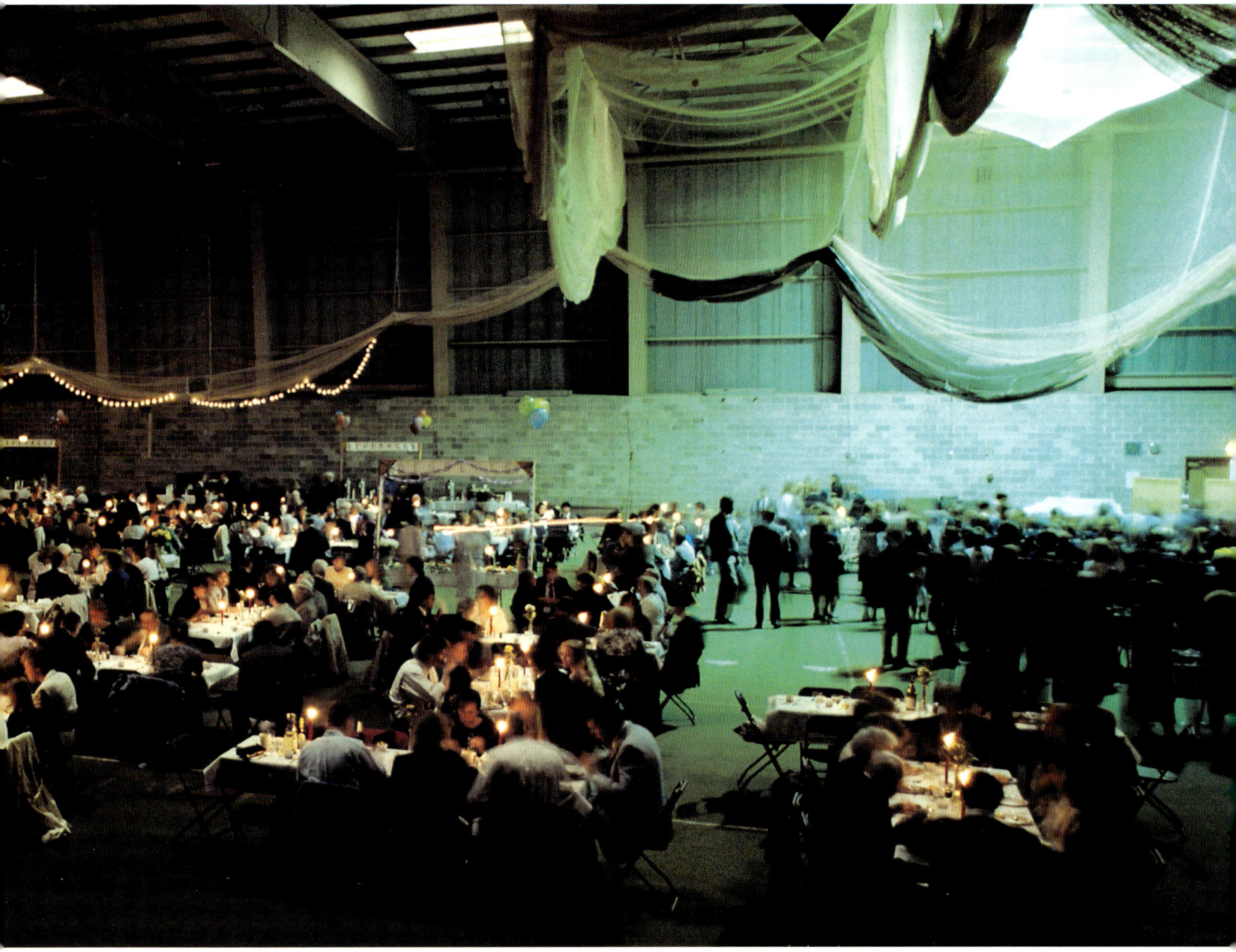

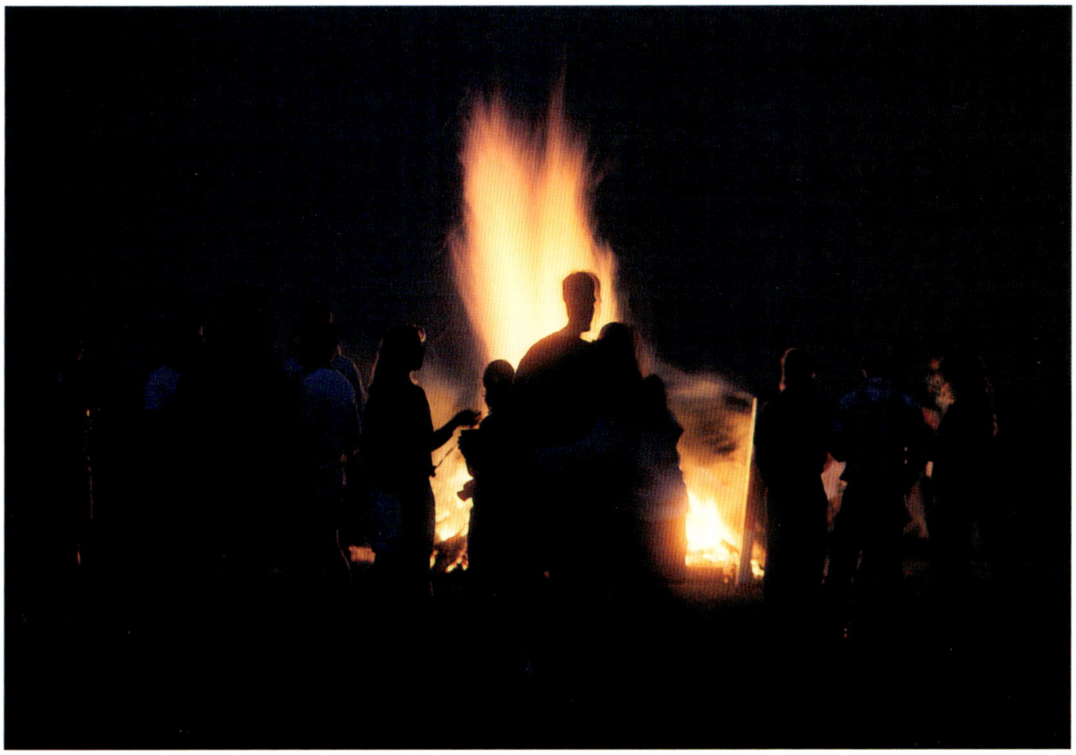

Alumni Reunion Parade

87

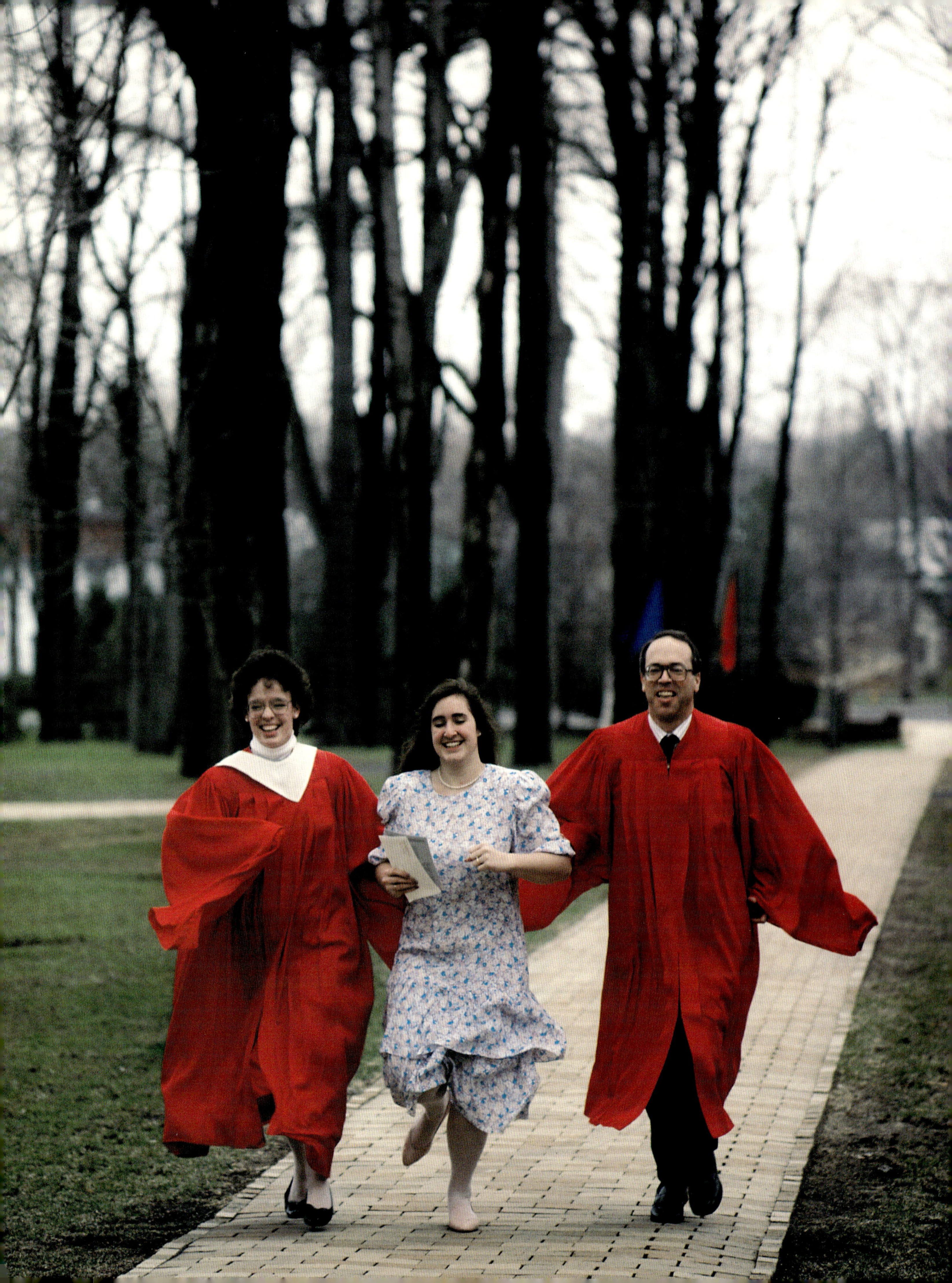

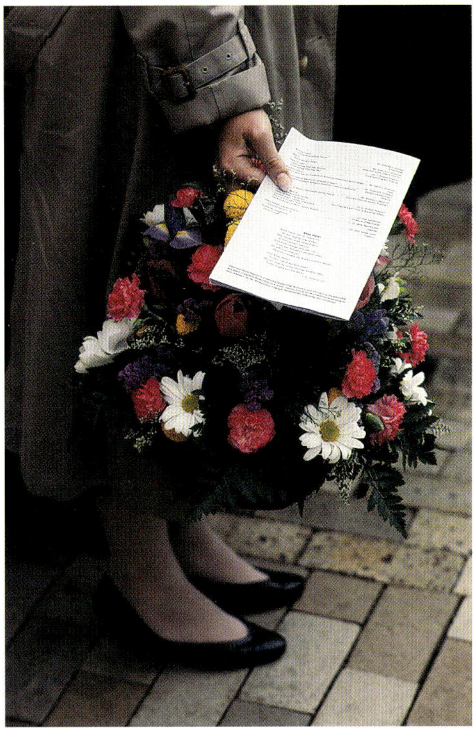

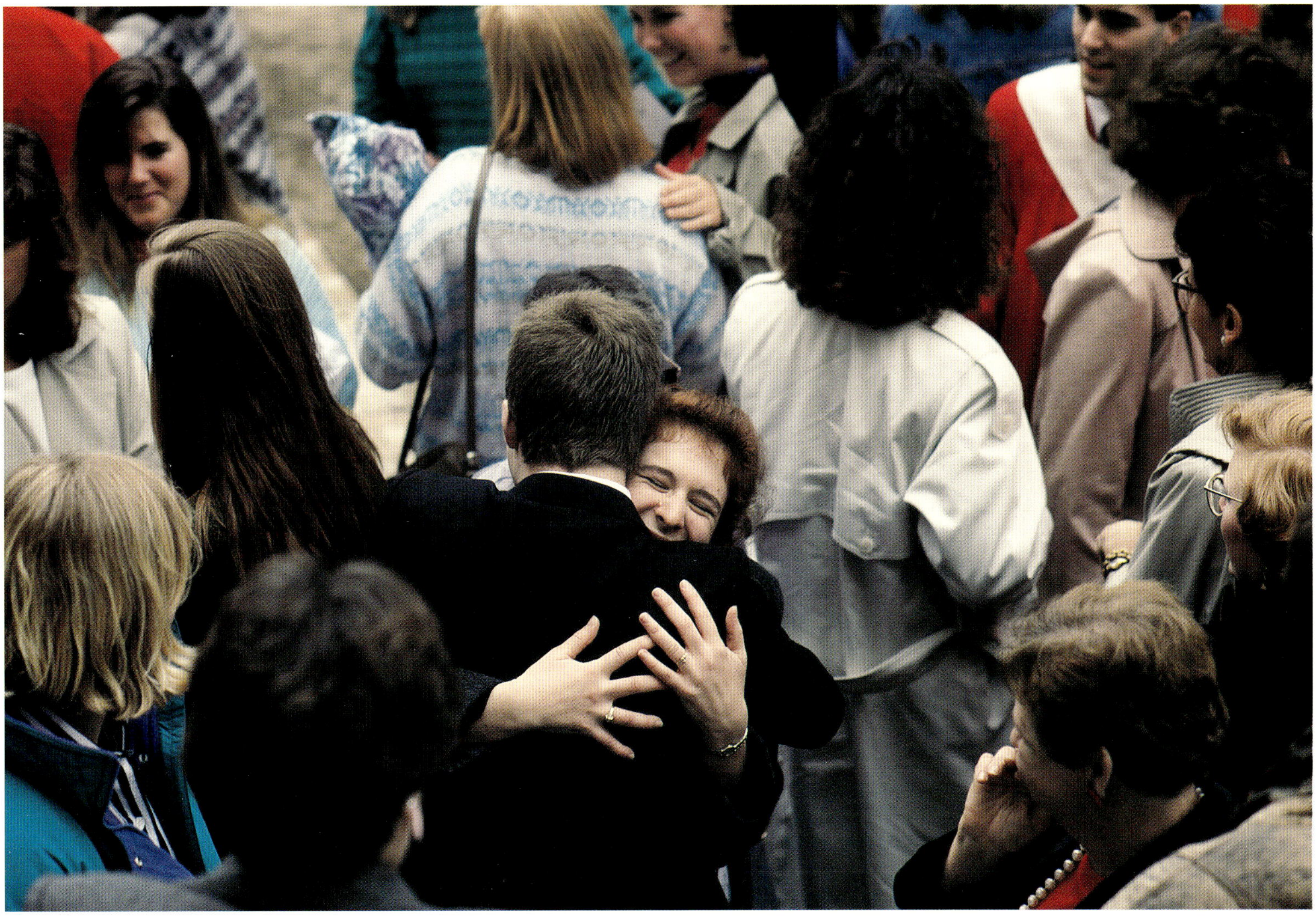

ROTC Commissioning Ceremony

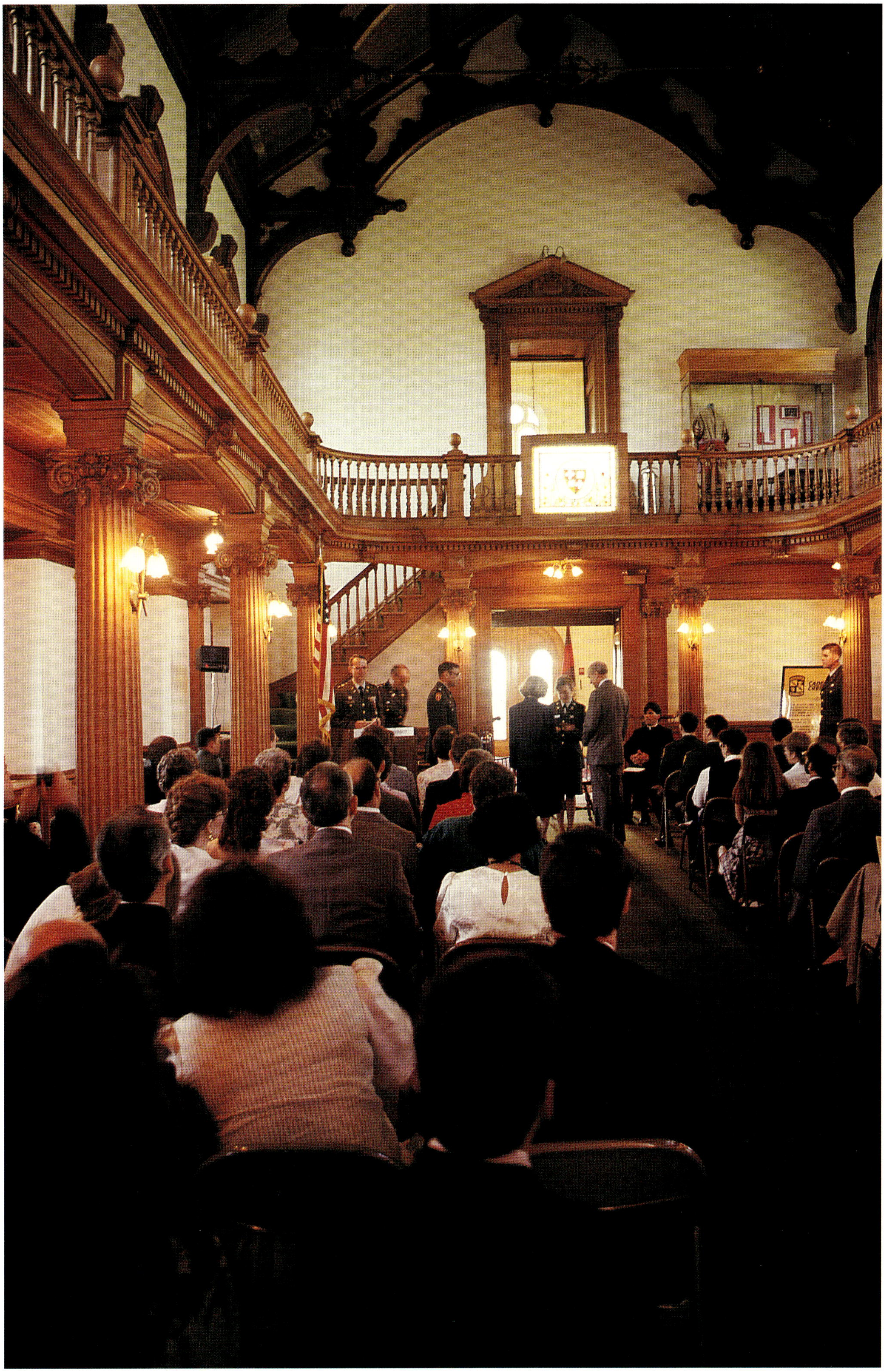

St. Lawrence University is part of the American heritage of independent institutions. There is nothing more important in the future of St. Lawrence than continued loyalty to that heritage. At the beginning it was said that the founding of St. Lawrence was the lighting of a candle in the wilderness. Since then, cities, towns, and villages have covered the area . . . There is not much left of the wilderness, but the need for light remains. If, at every succeeding century, it can be said, as we can say, of those who went before: "They kept the light shining" - the St. Lawrence story will be a treasured volume in the history of higher education.

Louis H. Pink/Rutherford E. Delmage in Candle in the Wilderness, 1956

93

94

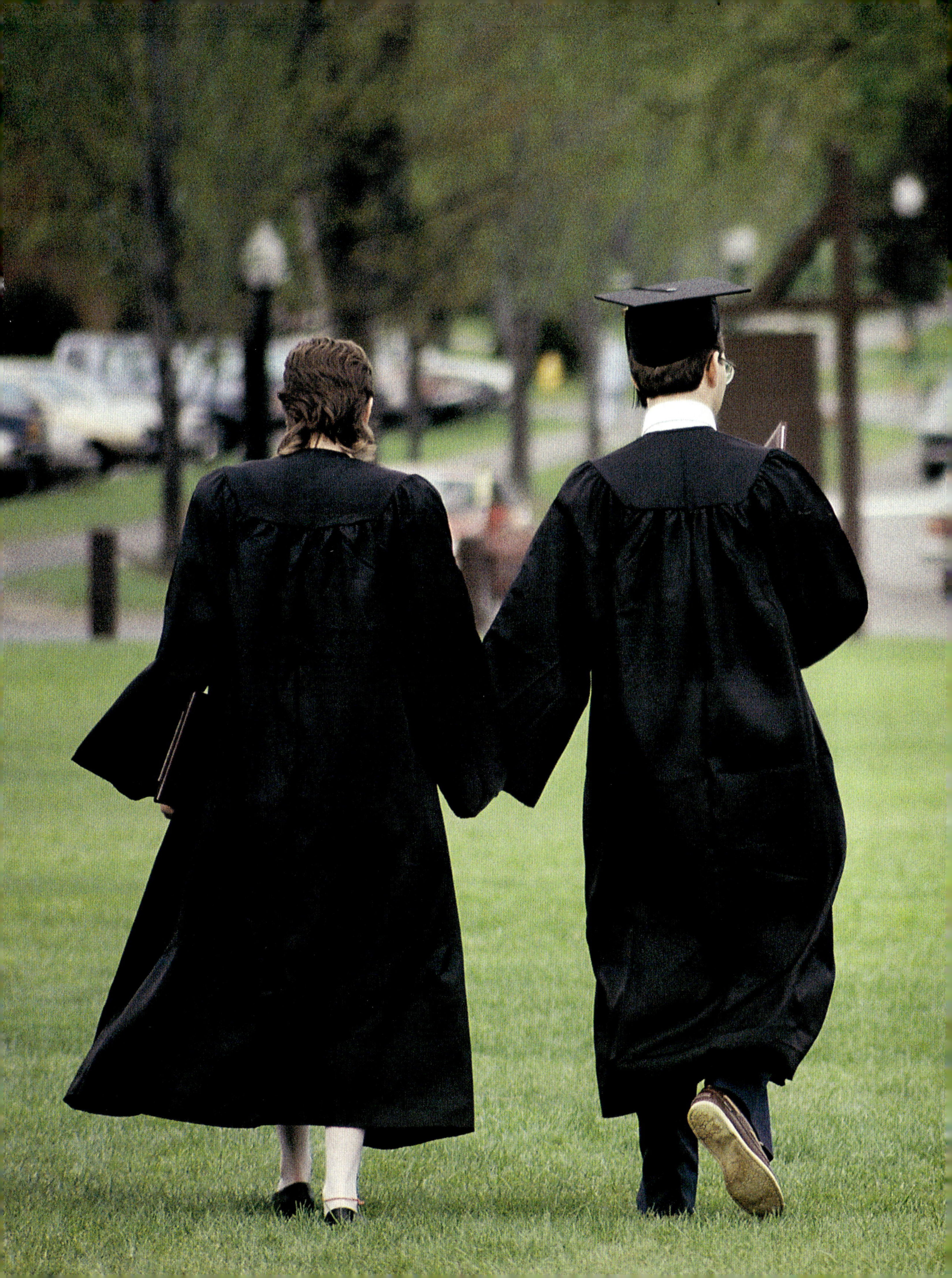

Fides et veritas

St. Lawrence Through The Years
A Backward Glance at St. Lawrence in Photographs from the Archives

In the 1890s three buildings comprised the St. Lawrence University campus: (from left) Richardson Hall, Fisher Hall and Herring Library.

The photographs on these pages show downtown Canton as it looked in the latter half of the 19th century. The town was the site of normal mercantile activity, but also provided the young university some off-campus diversion for students, and a town hall for commencement exercises and other large university gatherings (see photo bottom right).

(Left) Generations of students will remember arriving or departing by train from Canton Station (now the Hoot Owl). Here in 1947 students are boarding the "Holiday Special."

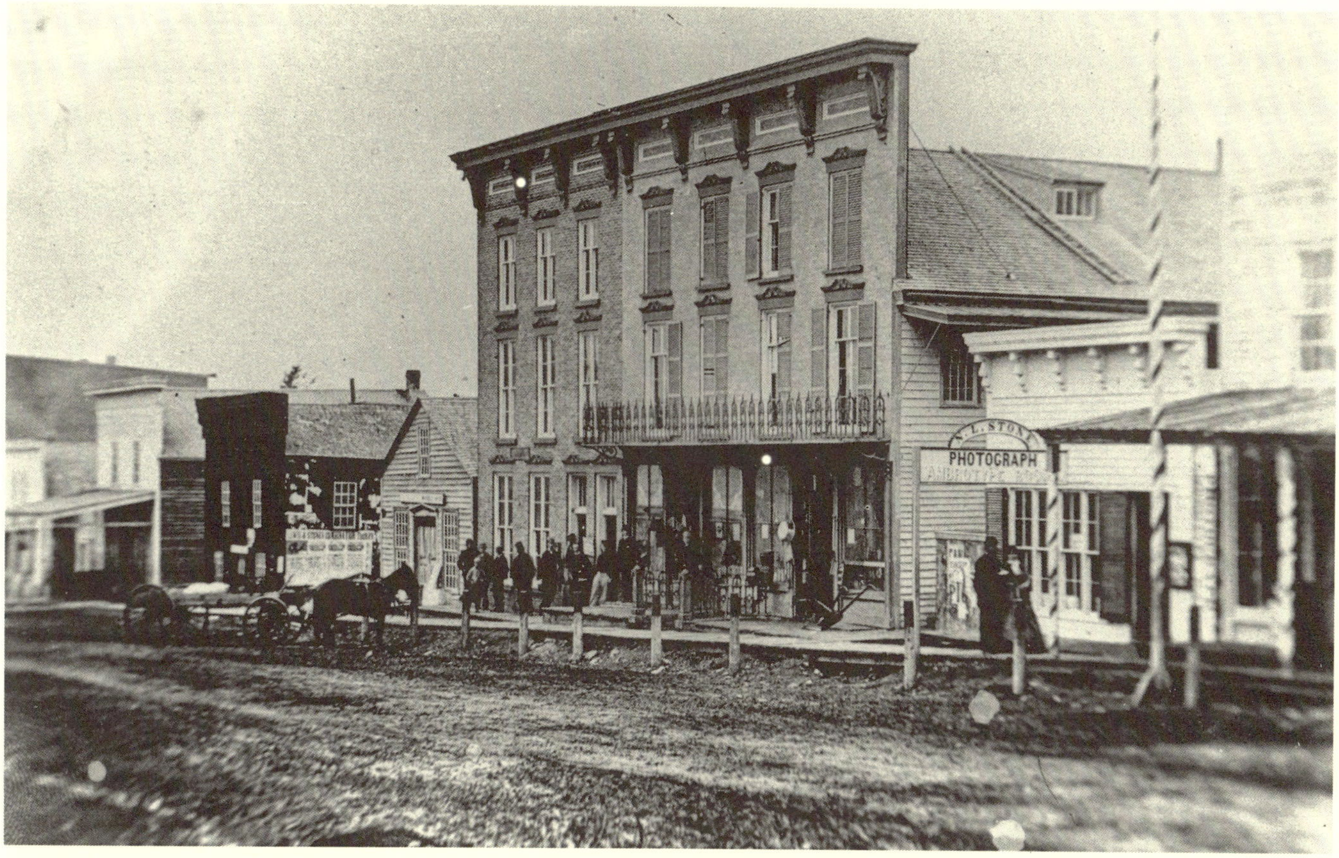
PHOTOGRAPH

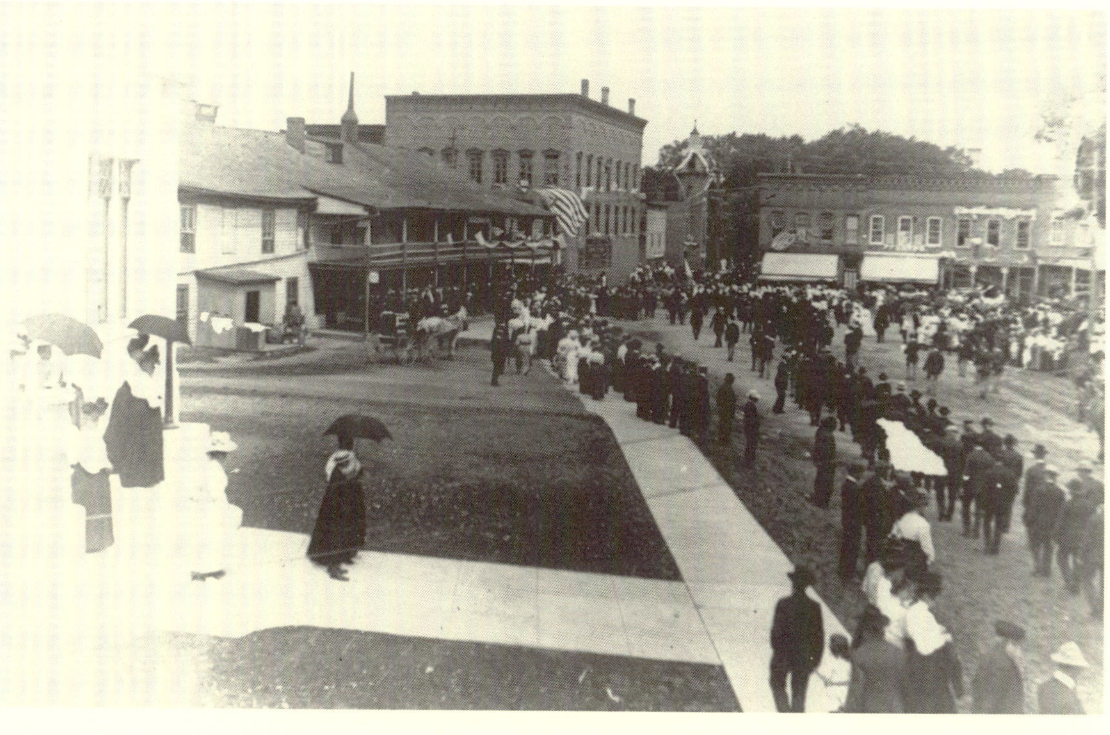

By 1909 the St. Lawrence campus had grown to this size. From left are: Fisher Hall, home of the Theological School; College Hall (now Richardson Hall); the Gymnasium; Carnegie Hall; the Beta House in its original location and Memorial Hall.

Thirty years later, in the late 1930s, the campus had grown significantly, as shown by the aerial photograph at right.

St. Lawrence University
(Skyview © by D. P. Church)

Park Street Hall, once President Gunnison's home, housed the University administration until 1962.

South Hall was a "temporary" classroom building behind Dean Eaton Residence Hall. It was built in 1949 to accommodate increased numbers of students after World War II. It was used until razed shortly after this picture was taken in 1968.

Carnegie Hall was the university's original science building, shown here in 1913. It was also used as a dormitory. The building was renovated in 1989, and now houses the Modern Languages and Literatures Department and International Education.

Dean Eaton Hall, soon after construction in 1927. The tower for WCAD, one of the first college radio stations in the U.S., is at right.

Above: The Weeks Athletic Field was crowded with fans for this sporting event in the early 1900s.

Right: The original Gymnasium on campus, shown here circa 1900, stood on the present-day site of Gunnison Chapel.

The Brewer Field House, 1949.

The ice hockey team in action in 1952 in Appleton Arena, two years after its construction.

105

The Great Ice Storm of March 27, 1913 damaged many of the trees on campus.

A Winter Carnival ice sculpture from the 1960s.

The Winter Carnival of 1936 featured a three-legged ski race.

The Owen D. Young Library now stands on the former site of the Gaines Theatre, shown here in the 1950s.

Dr. Charles M. Rebert taught at St. Lawrence from 1914 to 1951. He is shown here with his collie, Sandy.

An alumni luncheon at the men's dormitory, June 8, 1931.

Dr. Henry (Harry) Reiff was another faculty member whose career at St. Lawrence spanned several generations. He taught from 1928 to 1966.

President Absalom Gaines and his dog, Don, on Main Street in Canton, circa 1900. Gaines served as St. Lawrence's third president from 1872 to 1888. In the background is Town Hall, site of St. Lawrence's graduations until 1926, when the Gunnison Chapel became the location.

Commencement/Reunion, 1961. Commencements and Reunions were held simultaneously for many years.

Below: Commencement, 1930. From left are Dr. Richard E. Sykes, president from 1919-1935; Owen D. Young, chairman of the board from 1924-1933; Otis Skinner; and Nelson Robinson, Class of 1877.

Commencement, 1927.

110

Commencement, 1931.

In 1931, Commencement participants included, from left, Andrew W. Mellon, Owen D. Young and President Richard E. Sykes.

Outdoor graduation ceremonies are a St. Lawrence tradition, such as this one on Weeks Field in 1950.

The main walk to St. Lawrence University in the 1880s. Left to right are Herring Library, Richardson Hall and the Chapel (Fisher Hall).